For Cathryn Futral, this black hole in the literary ozone which will serve as a grim reminder of what can happen when the blood stops reaching a lawyer's brain.

Robert Legeell
12/91

MAIL FRAUD

The Laughable Letters of

ROBERT L. STEED

LONGSTREET PRESS
Atlanta, Georgia

Published by
LONGSTREET PRESS, INC.
2150 Newmarket Parkway
Suite 102
Marietta, Georgia 30067

Printed in the United States of America

1st printing 1991

Library of Congress Catalog Card Number: 90-061851

ISBN 0-929264-45-2

This book was printed by R. R. Donnelley & Sons, Harrisonburg, Virginia. The text was set in ITC American Typewriter Medium by Typo-Repro Service, Inc., Atlanta, Georgia.
Cover illustration by David Boyd

Editor's Note

Although it can't quite be said that this collection of the curious correspondence of Atlanta lawyer, columnist, humorist and cultural curmudgeon Robert L. Steed was published over his protest, it is fair to say that he was most reluctant to allow us to rummage through his personal files with a view toward a collection of letters.

We noted from casual discussions with various recipients of Steed's letters over the years, notably Tony Privett (former business manager to Lewis Grizzard) and David Boyd (syndicated political cartoonist), that many of them enjoyed Steed's quirky correspondence so much that they had preserved their own small collections of it. In fact, it was Privett who first suggested to us that a collection of Steed's letters would be worthwhile.

Steed's reluctance was overcome only after we reminded him that he could and should donate all of his proceeds from this book to his alma mater, Mercer University, as he has done with the proceeds of his four previous books, *Willard Lives!*, *Lucid Intervals*, *Money, Power and Sex (A Self-Help Guide for All Ages)* and *The Sass Menagerie*.

Steed's misgivings about this project are documented in the opening letter in this collection.

If we prove him wrong and this book enjoys the commercial success we believe it will, we may follow up with a collection of his trust indentures, lease agreements, demand letters and other legal writings and, if that proves successful, bring out a collection of his most creative writings of all—his federal income tax returns.

Dedication

*For my sassy secretary Yvonne
("that's not in my job description") McMillian
with boundless appreciation
for semi-loyal service since 1963.*

April 25, 1990

Mr. Claude (Just call me "Chuck") Perry
Maximum Publisher
Longstreet Press
Marietta, Georgia

Dear Claude:

I'm still very chary about a collection of letters by me. I can see towering stacks of remaindered books in stores across the land. However, this morning while Lu and I were on our regular pre-dawn walking foray into the mists, we gave some serious thought to titles for the collection of letters (actually, *I* gave some serious thought to the title; Lu simply heeled in a slack-jawed, narcoleptic trance trying to convince her wiry mind and body that they were still in bed). In any event, my latest entry in the Whatchagoncallit Handicap is *Mail Fraud: The Laughable Letters of Robert L. Steed.*

I like the *Mail Fraud* opening because it works on two levels. First, it suggests that there is something funny about the book, and second, it conveys my deeply held conviction that inflicting this literary dog's breakfast on an unsuspecting public is something which borders on criminality.

Beyond that, the *Laughable Letters of Robert L. Steed* seems good for a number of reasons: (i) it is straightforward and descriptive, (ii) the "laughable" conveys both "humorous" and a self-deprecating notion that the idea of publishing such clownish correspondence is, indeed, laughable, and (iii) it gets us around having a title which would then have to be followed with "by Robert L. Steed" which would seem awkward for a collection of letters.

As is always the case, too much serious analysis in matters of humor produces the same effect as saying a word over and over and over. After a while, nothing sounds right.

When Lu finally came to three-quarters of the way into our walk, she suggested *Sex, Lies and Measuring Tape,* which I rejected out of hand (whatever that means). However, it did give me an idea about a possible project for next year—the *Bob Steed, Jane Fonda Sex Tapes.* Of course, I would want to lose some weight before embarking on that project but, failing that, might consider appearing in a cut-out neoprene wet suit if Jane will go along. I'll have my people contact your people.

With warmest regards, I am

About to turn into the Uniroyal place to get my car serviced,

Robert L. Steed

March 9, 1988

Executive Committee
Lawyers Club of Atlanta, Inc.
Atlanta, Georgia

Gentlemen and Token Woman Executive Committee
Member, Ruth Tinsley West Garrett Brown (cha,
cha, cha):

Verley Spivey, an obscure member who slipped in
some years back when we did away with any pretense
of selectivity, will soon be proposing Ms. Lucy T.
Sheftall for membership in the Lawyers Club and this
letter is intended as a ringing endorsement of that
proposal. The fact that her proposer is at best lackluster should not suggest to you that Lucy would be anything other than a first-rate member of our burgeon-
ing society. I have enjoyed professional and social
contacts with her and assure you she will add luster to
our roster.

She is a *summa cum laude* graduate of the University of Georgia and a Virginia law graduate. She practiced three years with the McGuire, Woods and Battle
firm in Virginia and has been with the State Law
Department since June 1983.

More important, she falls squarely within our new
minority set-aside program established by the Executive Committee in an attempt to get more members
who were shorter and softer than Tom Watson Brown
and me. Well, she falls halfway: she's shorter than
both of us.

I commend her to you with much enthusiasm and hope you will give her proposal prompt and positive consideration.

Yours sincerely,

Robert L. Steed

P.S. Her husband, John M. Sheftall, is also a lawyer. Some on the Committee may be apprehensive that Lucy abandoned all feminist principles by taking his name. However, this is not so. He took her name. Before the marriage he was John M. Farquar and will, I believe, make an excellent and active member in our Spouse Auxiliary.

July 14, 1987

Mr. Ferber Buckley
Atlanta, Georgia

Dear Ferber:

Enclosed is my marker for $100 to the Citizens for Michael Lomax Committee covering all the shrimp you can eat for Robert L. and Linda R. (Lu) Steed. It is altogether appropriate that the affair has been deemed "low-country" as both adjectives fit you to a tee.

With best regards, I remain

Reasonably alert,

Robert L. Steed

March 21, 1988

Commissioner Tommy Irvin
Capitol Square
Atlanta, Georgia

Dear Tommy:

I noted in *Bill Shipp's Georgia* (he rejected the name I suggested for the newsletter— "Shipp Happens") that Senator Nunn, Speaker Murphy and you are in the seat-selling business. It sounds like a good idea to me and I am enclosing my check for $100. Please put my name on a wide one.

Yours sincerely,

Robert L. Steed

The following is a letter to UGA tennis coach Dan Magill regarding a roast of Coach Vince Dooley that he and Steed participated in on December 7, 1989.

December 13, 1989

Coach Dan Magill
Athens, Georgia

Dear Dan:

Thanks for your note and thanks too for being such a great roaster on Pearl Harbor Day. Coach Dooley may not have been the subject of a sneak attack, but I trust he felt thoroughly attacked before the evening was over. That reminds me of the story about a fellow who was half-black and half-Japanese. Every December 7 he had an uncontrollable urge to attack Pearl Bailey (and you thought I showed *no* restraint during the roast).

With best regards, I am

Yours sincerely,

Robert L. Steed

November 27, 1989

Mr. Robert L. Rearden, Jr.
President
Duncan Peek, Inc.
Atlanta, Georgia

Dear Roberto:

Knowing of and appreciating your growing collection of nicknames, I am enclosing two copies of an obituary written by a friend, Marianne Thomason of Newnan, regarding the demise of Rufus Jones, Jr., who crossed over Jordan's Stormy Banks earlier this month.

To get the point of the obits, you need only read the first paragraph of each. It turns out that the words in parentheses were not, as Ms. Thomason suspected, the cause of death. Rather, they were Rufus' sobriquet.

With warmest regards to you and all under your protection, I am

Just an old song nobody sings anymore,

Robert L. Steed

Original Copy	Corrected Copy
RUFUS JONES	**RUFUS JONES**
Rufus Jones, Jr., 74 Pinson Street, Newnan, passed away November 4, 1989 at the Medical College of Georgia in Augusta as a result of injuries received in an automobile accident.	Rufus (Car Wreck) Jones, Jr., 74 Pinson Street, Newnan, passed away November 4, 1989 at the Medical College of Georgia in Augusta.

December 18, 1989

Mr. J. L. Levine
Managing Director
Investment Banking
Dean Witter Reynolds Inc.
Atlanta, Georgia

Dear Jay:

Thanks very much for the handsome 1990 calendar.

It is great looking and smells good (but then the same can be said for most of the waiters at those restaurants in Buckhead).

I'm a bit put off every time I look at the gold emblazoned 1990 on its cover and realize with renewed clarity that the shadows are indeed getting longer.

Yours sincerely,

Robert L. Steed

The following is a thank-you note from Steed to a friend who sent a photo of Steed making a speech.

January 17, 1989

J. David Parrish, Esq.
Hurt & Parrish
Orlando, Florida

Dear David:

What a double-barreled treat—first a sweet note from Esta and then the glossy 8x10 from you.

While I'll have to agree that you had a great keynote speaker, you need to give serious consideration to getting a new cameraman. The one you had—through faulty equipment, bad focus and poor angle—made me look overweight. In fact, the knot of my necktie is 90% obscured by what would appear to be a dangling wattle. I know the unsophisticated say that the camera never lies, but without some serious explanation others seeing this photo might think your keynote speaker was Charles Laughton.

With best regards, I am

Increasingly jowly,

Robert L. Steed

Steed's humor columns in the Atlanta Constitution *often provoke responses from strange pen pals. Barry Newman of Buchanan, Georgia, has been, according to Steed, one of the most interesting and enduring.*

January 31, 1990

Hon. Barry Newman
Unlicensed Whittler and
  Resident Philosopher
Buchanan, Georgia

Dear Barry:

Thanks for taking my pulse by mail. The vital signs are faint but not flat.

As to interesting things happening with me, I can report that I spoke to the Bowdon Boosters Club evening before last on the occasion of their celebration of being runner-up in the State football championship (Division A). I was co-captain of the 1953 squad (primarily because it was my football) and distinguished myself as a triple threat man ("run, stumble and fall"). The 1953 team was the beginning of a football revival at Bowdon as the sport hadn't been played there since the early 30s. Some said it wasn't played in 1953 either, but we had a good time and I was glad to see some of my old teammates at the banquet. We didn't have face masks back then and I could sure tell it looking at my old teammates.

I am interested in your proposed book on the undertaking business. I like the title but you might also consider, *"We'll be the Last Ones to Let You Down."* Your participation with the local undertaker may give new meaning to the term "ghost writer."

The type in your letter looks awfully familiar. You didn't buy the typewriter in Enterprise, Alabama, by any chance did you? I just wanted to know because if you did, I want to be sure my secretary opens all of your mail in the future.

With best regards, I am

Sitting up and taking nourishment,

Robert L. Steed

Postcard from Rome to Barbara Mendel, New York City:
(10-13-82)

Veni, Vedi,
Shopi, Eati.

Bob

Steed's newspaper columns often provoke hostile letters to the editor. The following is a response to one such letter which commented on his obvious girth.

February 1, 1988

Ms. Maya G. White
Atlanta, Georgia

Dear Ms. White:

Your smoking submission of December 21, 1987, to *The Atlanta Constitution*, has just been forwarded to me. I think the editors, fearful of provoking the Battered Columnist Syndrome, attempt to spare my fragile ego by putting some time between the publication of this type letter and actually sending the original to me.

Your letter is a master work and shows great insight. However, you were fooled by the photograph that they run with my column. Actually, I am tall, dark, unbespectacled and lean as a whippet. Because the column is supposed to be a humor column, the editors choose to run what they think is a humorous photo. It is, in fact, a picture of a not-so-famous character actor who appeared in many movies during the 30s and 40s—"Cuddles" Sakal. Aside from that, you were right on the button. . . .

With warm regards, I am

Yours sincerely,

Robert L. Steed

July 30, 1987

Mr. George B. Ramsay, Jr.
McClure, Ramsay & Dickerson
Toccoa, Georgia

Dear Cousin Boots:

I appreciate the individual announcement of your new associate and am delighted to see that the feminist movement has spread to the hinterlands. After long experience, we have absolutely no doubt that women make first-rate lawyers and as Ralph Waldo Emerson (I think it was Emerson, it could have been Howard Cosell), once said:

"If you think that Fred Astaire was great, just remember that Ginger Rogers did everything he did backwards and in high heels."

With best regards, I am

Yours sincerely,

Robert L. Steed

Steed's long-time friend and client, Rod Frazer, was the subject of what Steed thought to be an excessively laudatory profile in The Piedmont [Alabama] Journal. *This was Steed's response. Remarkably, Frazer remains a friend and client.*

January 27, 1987

Mr. Nimrod T. Frazer
("Known nationally and internationally
in the highest financial circles")
The Frazer Lanier Company, Inc.
Montgomery, Alabama

Dear Mr. Frazer:

Sources close to me in the newspaper business forwarded to me your recent profile in the January 21, 1987 issue of *The Piedmont Journal*. It gives new meaning to the phrase "That would gag a maggot."

I know that in the Kingdom of the Blind, a one-eyed man would be King, but you have really done a job on those rustics in Piedmont, Alabama (pop. 5,544). You have obviously blown so much smoke up their nether regions that they must be going around looking like the Alabama equivalents of blackened redfish.

I don't know what you did to the fellow who wrote the piece but it must have been sufficiently obscene to cause him not to attach his byline to the story. In fact, the photo that accompanied the article looked like someone who, after a great deal of soul searching, finally decided to come out of the closet at the Walter

Jenkins Room of the YMCA. Was that a scarf around your neck or a colostomy bag trying to get out of your collar? I thought at first it was a paisley goiter but I don't think the author would have been so rhapsodic in the face of such a grisly physical defect. If you and he ever break up, promise you'll give back the ring.

I see from the early paragraphs that the anonymous author of this paroxysm of praise got to see your tattered battle citation. Frankly, after reading the piece, I am baffled as to why we didn't win in Korea with you in the lineup.

Of all the ringing self-aggrandizement throughout the article, the comment by Lamar Lovejoy was the one which most severely taxed my gag reflex. You obviously had that poor yokel in a state of dazed stupefaction to provoke him into slobbering "He is one of the smartest financiers I have ever talked to, and I have talked to some of the best. He's brilliant." When they finally let Mr. Lovejoy out of the Alabama State Home for the Easily Impressed, I'd like to talk to him about some property I have in West Georgia which I think could be snapped up at a reasonable price for high rise office buildings. I am almost embarrassed to mention this as my suggestion is obviously profit-motivated, unlike the sheer altruism which permeates all of your activities in the Piedmont region.

How, a dazed world wonders, did this Alabama backwater get to be the beneficiary of Nimrod Frazer's entrepreneurial daring? I supposed the Piedmontese should not look a gift horse in the mouth (or in any other aperture) but it is a bit mysterious as to why they were singled out for your selfless and staggering leadership.

I think the least these bright-eyed boosters could do is to erect a statue on the square in your honor. I see you dressed in a toga bearing shafts of grain (symbolizing prosperity and progress) in one hand and a bag of fertilizer (symbolizing your chief personality trait) in the other. If you are too busy with your national and international travels to pose for the piece, I believe we could get Charlton Heston to stand in. As you know, Chill Wills passed away. At the base of the monument I would suggest something dignified but simple, perhaps along the following lines—"What he's done for others, he can do for you."

With warmest regards, I am

> Still having trouble swallowing,
>
> Robert L. Steed

July 21, 1988

Mr. Al Dempsey
Martinez, Georgia

Dear Al:

I'm sorry I can't come to the steak dinner to kick off your re-election campaign, but my wizened bride of thirty years is returning from Africa and will expect me to be spending some time with her to hear all of her stories.

I am enclosing a check to show that my heart (if not my big bottom) is in the right place. I would have sent more but as Joe Kennedy once told Jack, "I'll be damned if I'm going to pay for a landslide."

Good luck.

Yours sincerely,

Robert L. Steed

February 21, 1990

President
Victoria's Secret
North American Office
Columbus, Ohio

Dear Sir or Madam:

I thought you might be interested in a recent column of mine published on the op-ed page of *The Atlanta Constitution*. It deals with the growing plague of mail order catalogs. However, as you will see from the column, I draw a line between the mountains of catalogs offering an incredible assortment of useless items and those which provide a worthy service to the community like Victoria's Secret.

Also enclosed is an earlier column which includes a reference to Victoria's Secret.

One of my friends suggested to me that with all this laudatory praise I have been generating for your fine company that I should be entitled to something in return. However, looking through your catalog (which I do rigorously and regularly if my wife doesn't beat me to the mailbox and hide it from me) I can't find anything in my size — 44 Fat.

However, I would be more than content to have an autographed photo of my favorite model and, hoping that you will be persuaded that I have earned it, I am enclosing a copy of her photo from your catalog.

Keep up the good work. Your catalog does more to get my heart jump-started than freebasing chicory and caffeine-loaded coffee.

With best regards, I am

Easily aroused,

Robert L. Steed

March 15, 1990

Ms. Cynthia A. Fedus
President and Chief Executive Officer
Victoria's Secret Catalogue
North American Office
New York, New York

Dear Cynthia:

You're a sweetheart if there ever was one! Thanks so much for taking the trouble to answer my recent letter and to pass along my heartfelt request to the Unknown, and almost Unclad, Model.

Please assure her that my request was not the literary equivalent of an obscene phone call and that I can furnish certification from my wife that I am virtually harmless.

In ringing proof of the eternal verity of the maxim that "No good deed goes unpunished," I am enclosing for you with my warmest compliments a collection of columns so that you will never be tempted to subscribe to the *Constitution*. I would urge you not to read too many of these at one sitting as permanent damage can result to your literary gag reflex.

As an added inducement to the Model-in-Question, you may assure (or perhaps threaten) her that I would love to send along a copy to her as well when I have her name. This is beginning to sound like one of those personal ads in the back of the *New York Magazine* (SFL [short, fat, lawyer] seeks autographed photo of sloe-eyed, lanky and lovely model for purposes of filling scrapbook and jump-starting heart).

With renewed thanks for being such a pleasant good sport, I am

Breathing heavily,

Robert L. Steed

February 12, 1990

Mr. Johnny B. Lastinger
Head Knocker
Valdosta-Lowndes Chamber of Commerce
Valdosta, Georgia

Dear Johnny B.:

I am sorry that I did not make the Bird Supper last evening.

Lu and I had made plans to attend and had held the evening open for that purpose. (Now comes the incredible part of my excuse.)

Our son, Josh Steed, had given us a hot air balloon trip and it was scheduled for Saturday afternoon. However, the wind and rains which blew through caused it to be put over until Sunday afternoon, but we were assured that we would finish up in time to permit us to get on the outside of some of those South Georgia game birds. I had never been lied to before by a hot air balloonist, so I had no reason to suspect these assurances.

At 6:30 last evening when the sun was down, we were up . . . in that damned hot air balloon soaring south somewhere near Lovejoy. The pilot, in a voice as-calm-as-could-be, said, "Well, we have run out of light and we're running out of fuel so we'd better look for a place to put this thing down. I want all of you to watch out for power lines." As you might imagine, this caused every orifice in my ample body to snap shut as three-fifths of the Swiss Family Steed was on board.

We finally (and mercifully) landed in something of a controlled crash on a pipeline right-of-way and spent the next two hours (1) whimpering with relief; (2) helping Captain Hot Air deflate and repack the balloon; (3) finding our launch site where an automobile of one of the fliers had been abandoned; and (4) winding our weary way home.

We didn't get there until about 9:30 and figured all of your goodies were gone.

The purpose of all this elaborate explanation is to insure that we will be on next year's invitation list and to assure you that we continue to appreciate being invited.

With warmest regards to you and all under your protection, I am

Still a little giddy,

Robert L. Steed

September 9, 1988

Mr. Robert W. Dhue
President
Atlanta Coliseum, Inc.
The Omni
Atlanta, Georgia

Dear Bob:

Enclosed is my marker for two tickets to the Frank Sinatra deal on September 22. It seemed like the only civilized thing to do given the fact that my highly paid secretary recoiled in horror at the ticket price for her dear old mother. I'm sure her mother would not have blanched so at the price as she is a well-to-do cosmetologist in South Cobb County and lives in a unique underground bunker there which has been featured in the newspapers. She does, however, come out on Groundhog Day and for Frank Sinatra concerts.

It will be my pleasure to treat her and a consenting adult of her choice to this concert.

I'll be back in touch regarding the Prince tickets. Thanks.

Until then, I am

Subject to wild mood swings,

Robert L. Steed

To the children from
Barcelona, Spain:
(6-22-90)

If Lu doesn't stop stuffing herself, she'll never get back in the U.S. on her old passport.

Bob

In response to a request for a copy of a popular column on telephone manners, Steed offered the following.

October 11, 1988

Mr. Mike Faherty
WSB Radio
Atlanta, Georgia

Dear Mike:

Enclosed is a copy of the column on telephone manners which I hope will be useful to you.

I still think the premise is correct but must admit that there are frequent colloquies between my secretary, Yvonne "That File's Been Lost for Years" McMillian, and me along the following lines:

Me:	"Who is this Farqhuar guy who called?"
McMillian:	"How should I know?"
Me:	"Who is he with?"
McMillian:	"Beats hell out of me."
Me:	"Well, do you know what he wants?"
McMillian:	"No, don't you remember, you told me not to ask all that stuff." (This line delivered with a certain amount of smugness.)

With best regards, I remain

On hold,

Robert L. Steed

Steed, ever creative, offers one of the all-time best excuses for a bounced check. He swears it's true.

November 4, 1988

Macy Skinner
Campaign Treasurer
Richard Ray
U.S. Congress
Perry, Georgia

Dear Macy:

I am sorry my check to the Congressman's campaign bounced. My wife was vacationing in Kenya and her pocketbook (and checkbook) were stolen in Nairobi and we had to close the account and open a new one.

A replacement check is enclosed with my apologies for the confusion.

With best regards, I am

Yours sincerely,

Robert L. Steed

The following is Steed's response to an announcement by two of his Mercer University law school mates announcing their new partnership.

April 6, 1988

Mr. John Milton Harrison
Harrison, Hicks & Hicks
Eastman, Georgia

Mr. John H. Hicks
Harrison, Hicks & Hicks
Dublin, Georgia

Gentlemen:

I note with trepidation and great dismay the news of your malodorous union. With the possible exception of the joining of the axis forces in World War II, I would venture to say that there has scarcely been a combination that posed a more serious threat to the social order than the one you now propose to undertake.

Not content with having thoroughly disgraced the reputation of the Milton Clark Barwick Award for its more worthy recipients, you two have engaged in a history of multiple marriages, sharp practicing, heavy drinking on the part of one of you (and you know who you are), and self-mutiliation with a power saw on the part of the other (we all know who you are). Your respective contributions to the law to date would not fill a thimble but it has always been the hope and belief of the organized Bar that acting separately you posed no serious threat to the community. Now, however, the malevolent potential promised by the two of you acting in concert is a grisly and bitter business. Even more dangerous is the fact that you have obviously gulled some young and unsuspecting practitioner to join you and thus have access to the law through the labors of his research activities.

That the illegitimate son of Van Heflin and Carmen Miranda would join forces with a three-fingered pettifogger who abandoned the practice for ten years to fritter away the resources of his formerly rich wife in a life of maritime idleness and self-indulgence is a prospect which would test the gag reflex of a maggot inspector.

My best guess is that the two of you will soon pop up on cable television in Middle Georgia attempting to foist your dubious talents off on an unsuspecting and unsophisticated populace. You both are ringing proof of the maxim that no one is completely worthless; you can always serve as a bad example.

This is a black day for the Bar.

With serious apprehensions, I am

Thoroughly disgusted,

Robert L. Steed

December 9, 1988

Mr. David Morgan
Oglethorpe Power Company
Tucker, Georgia

Dear David:

What a great gift! Thanks to you and all my friends
at Oglethorpe for keeping me on your list. The
calculator-pen and pad set is outstanding. I borrow
tons of money and pay tons of interest (almost no
principal) to Trust Company Bank every year and they
give me a cheesy little vinyl calendar which I would be
embarrassed to take out inside the perimeter.
Come to see me. Until then, I remain

Reasonably alert,

Robert L. Steed

Miguel:

The high point of the trip for all of us has been to see the actual 1951 Chevrolet in which Caesar Romero brutally deflowered Sandra Dee in "Kiss My Garbonza." Our guide couldn't tell us anything about the other car. We're having a great time, but Lu is still feeling a little guilty about leaving the kids at the Ramada Inn in Beaumont, Texas.

Bob

March 20, 1987

Executive Committee
Lawyers Club of Atlanta
Atlanta, Georgia

Gentlemen:

Lawyer Verley Spivey, Esq., is proposing my friend Grace E. Evans for membership in the Lawyers Club and the purpose of this note is to enthusiastically second that proposal.

I am going to say it to you straight. We need Grace Evans in the Lawyers Club. I spoke to the Club night before last and I have never seen a more grisly looking bunch in my life. About half of them looked as though they would have paid to see a root canal. What is badly needed in that rag-tag assemblage is some beauty, charm and (no pun intended) grace, and lawyer Evans fills the bill in splendid measure on all counts.

Aside from being bright, attractive and well spoken, Lawyer Evans is one of the few University of Georgia law graduates I know who can consistently put a noun against a verb and form a complete sentence. This, of course, is attributable solely to the fact that she graduated from Mercer University in 1973 with a B.A. in English.

More important, she is, unlike so many of that lowing herd of practitioners who form the motley and monthly stampede for free food and drink, one familiar with the inside of a courtroom . . . .

She is a fine person, an excellent lawyer and would add considerable luster to our roster. I urge that you give Mr. Spivey's proposal your prompt and positive consideration.

With warmest regards, I am

Resting comfortably,

Robert L. Steed

December 15, 1988

Mr. James H. Groome
Atlanta, Georgia

Dear Jim:

I'm sad to report that when I checked with Lamar Manufacturing Company in Bowdon the houndstooth sports jacket you admired was not in stock in any size, particularly, as they pointed out, a size as popular as 40 regular.

I'm sorry I couldn't turn it up for you as I was planning to charge a small commission for myself. However, you should know that many see outfits on me and think that if they get the outfit they will look just as good as I do. They are almost always disappointed.

With best regards, I am

Dapper as ever,

Robert L. Steed

The following is a letter to Steed's long-time friend Nolan Murrah, who took early retirement as an officer of the Royal Crown Company to grow mangoes on Captiva Island, Florida. It refers to their mutual friend, the late Martelle Layfield, who was an early volunteer for Presidential candidate George Bush.

November 18, 1988

Mr. Nolan Murrah
Former Vice President, Secretary
  and General Counsel
Now Southwest Florida's Mysterious
  "Mango Man"
Captiva Island, Florida

Dear Asa:

Whaddayasaysa?

I'm sure the Republican victory bells are pealing in southwest Florida.

That's all those retired mouth-breathers from the Midwest who migrate down there in such appalling numbers can think of—protecting the Social Security benefits and making sure that Congress continues to vote whopping subsidies to prune growers. Perhaps if you played up the cathartic properties of mangoes, you could get in on some of that Department of Agriculture largesse as well.

Layfield is already attempting to exploit his Bush connections. Word has it that he is being considered for Postmaster provided he is willing to relocate to

Cusseta. I worry about the problems with confirmation. As you know, the FCC is still investigating charges that he has been pirating cable television by standing in his back yard with his ears wrapped in tin foil. I can't speak to those charges from any personal knowledge but I do know that he is *always* quoting Dr. Ruth on something or other.

Layfield keeps me posted on your doings. He says that the mangoes are covering Captiva with the vigor and relentlessness of Kudzu and that you are warmly regarded and widely respected by the local rustics who think you are the illegitimate offspring of a random but historic coupling between Ernest Hemingway and Margaret Chase Smith (which would, I imagine, explain both your appearance and your politics).

I guess this will teach you to write me a letter; you never can tell when somebody will answer those things.

Give my love to Barbara and all others under your protection and know that I remain

> Politically inept,
>
> Robert L. Steed

41

November 17, 1988

Mr. L. Martelle Layfield, Jr.
Layfield & Rothschild
Columbus, Georgia

Dear Martelle:

I have had good intentions but no follow through on my resolve to write you a letter congratulating you on the Bush Sweep. Though the newspapers assure me that it is not a mandate (apparently more than 40 states out of 50 is required), I think it's a pretty handy win and wanted to snuggle up to you as quickly as possible with the thought that you might be useful to me later when I am being considered for some high appointed government post.

I know your chillun were pleased with the results. Quayle apparently wasn't the albatross the national press declared him to be. However, I think he needs to mature some. They say in Bush strategy sessions that if anyone lights a cigarette, Quayle always begs to blow out the match.

As for you, I don't care what sort of post you take as long as you don't give up any legal representations of entities which have the capacity to incur debt and issue bonds.

With congratulations and warmest good wishes, I am

Thinking only of myself,

Robert L. Steed

December 30, 1988

Robert B. McCord, Jr., Esq.
Hapeville, Georgia

Dear Bob:

I certainly didn't take umbrage (my doctor took me off umbrage almost three years ago) at your comments about my having concubines in several nearby towns. I must tell you, however, that a couple of the concubines were a little pushed out of shape about your flip remarks. The fact is they simply revere me and, based on my performances, who can blame them?

Keep buying the books; I'd like to stay on the Best Seller List as long as I can and it's multiple purchasers like you who are priming the pump. In fact, I thought about titling the book *"Multiple Sarcasms"* but my wiry bride thought it too sexual.

With warmest regards, I remain

Easily insulted,

Robert L. Steed

January 25, 1989

J. William Pierce, Jr., Esq.
Memphis, Tennessee

Dear Will:

Thanks so very much for your kind note of January 24. It is a happy and generous thought you offer to the effect that I might be responsible for your success. However inaccurate and overly generous that might be, I certainly appreciate the thought.

It makes me think of a story that I sometimes use on myself in speaking engagements.

I say that in a sentimental moment I once said to my friend and mentor, Judge Griffin B. Bell, "Judge, what would you say if I told you that of all the people who have influenced me, you are the one most responsible for what I am today?"

The Judge considered the statement for a few moments and then replied, "Well, I guess I'd just have to learn to live with it."

I am happy to live with the notion that my recommendation to Mercer Law School might have been a proximate cause of your being where you are today. I would give it a one-half of one percent contribution. The balance being the result of the fact that you were, to borrow a Ferrol Sams phrase, "raised right." You have two great parents.

With warmest regards, I am

Yours sincerely,

Robert L. Steed

November 27, 1989
Mr. Santford W. Martin
Atlanta, Georgia

Dear Mr. Martin:

Thanks so much for your very nice letter of November 6, 1989, which was grudgingly forwarded to me by the *Atlanta Constitution*.

You may know that I, too, "many, many years ago hacked a little copy for a little college weekly newspaper"—the *Mercer Cluster*. It was, in fact, the journalistic incubator for the likes of those who later became real newspapermen such as Bert Struby (the publisher of the *Macon News and Telegraph*), Jack Tarver and Reg Murphy. (You may remember that Reg Murphy left town in the trunk of an automobile. They were going to get Jack Tarver but he wouldn't fit in the automobile trunk.)

I genuinely appreciate your taking the time to write me and your promise (it was a promise wasn't it?) to buy a copy of *The Sass Menagerie* (Longstreet Press, $14.95 in hardback and available at fine bookstores everywhere).

With best regards, I am

Easily encouraged,

Robert L. Steed

P. S. Did you know someone put a "T" in your first name?

Miguel —

As you can see from this photo,
the Mexican police have taken a
somewhat novel approach to
the problem of homosexuals.
The photo shows a special
police squad known as the
"Gay Caballeros." If they
uncover any such activity, they
flog the offenders silly with
those palm fronds. Everyone
seems to love it.

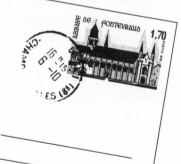

Yo' Bro'

Bob

March 6, 1989

Mr. and Mrs. Billy Thomasson
Newnan, Georgia

Dear Marianne and Billy:

As you could doubtless tell from the dent I made in your Irish Whiskey, I had a mighty good time at your country redoubt Saturday evening. I am authorized to say that Senora Steed had a good time as well but, as she is so easily entertained, this is not something you would want to note in your Guest Book.

I think it is worth noting that Michael, David and I, who together have less to offer in the way of interesting experiences than Dave Kindred, managed to keep him out of the conversation almost totally except for one brief interlude when he managed to elbow his way in with some anecdotal material about Muhammed Ali. I hope that after we left Mike and David either talked themselves out or drank themselves quiet, giving Brother Kindred a moment or two at the podium. Otherwise, the food, company and hospitality were all great, and Lu and I were delighted to be included.

We were both shocked and sorry to see that last evening's tornado whipped through the Newnan No-Tell Motel and hope that no one was in residence who wasn't supposed to be.

With warmest regards, I remain

Hungry for affection,

Robert L. Steed

February 22, 1989

Mr. John R. Harrison
President
New York Times Regional
   Newspaper Group
Atlanta, Georgia

Dear Smilin' Jack:

Enclosed is an exposition on just one of the swift and cunning thoughts coursing through my brain or, as Lu says, "cursing through my brain."

Maybe you could get the New York Times to put a bounty on me because of my books. Lu suggests that the book needs no help in getting removed from the shelves at Waldens or B. Daltons.

Speaking of Lu (and I note that I have spoken of her twice in this very short letter, a frequency bordering on obsession), she is still grinding (though exceedingly slow) on your portrait. She blocked out this entire week to finish it but was felled with a particularly virulent flu which will likely fuzz her ability to complete it within the next few days. However, it is well along the way, and though I am prejudiced about the artist and the subject, I like it very much.

With warmest regards, I am

Eager to offend,

Robert L. Steed

AS I SAT IN the green room of a local television station awaiting an opportunity to go on the air to flog my latest book, (*The Sass Menagerie*, $12.95 hardback, available at fine book stores everywhere or, for orders or two or more, I'll come out to your house, apartment, or doublewide and sign anything in that sucker you want), it occurred to me that there must be a better way to spur book sales than this approach. I was even more firmly convinced when I only had a two-minute sliver of time and was followed by a ferret from the Atlanta Zoo who got five minutes even though he couldn't talk. When I testily made this observation to the anchor man after the show, he said, "That's why the ferret got more time."

Driving back to the office from the interview, a sudden surge of blood reached my brain and the ultimate solution to hyping book sales occurred to me with blinding clarity. That is, of course, to get the Ayatollah Khomeini to publicly condemn the book and threaten my life or, preferably, the lives of my publishers, Simon & Lipschutz (New York, Philadelphia and Austell). Why hadn't I thought of that in the first place?

When the Great One, in his role as Exalted Literary Critic, hurled bans at the recently published *Satanic Verses* by Salman Rushdie, sales went off the charts. There was, of course, a dark side to the publicity in that the Ayatollah offered $5,200,000 to anyone who would send Rushdie to that great Autograph Party in the Sky. I confess right up front that I would be a little intimidated about this aspect of the program, but for a real rush in book sales, I would be willing to have my wife start my car every morning for a year or so.

Attempting to put that pale thought to vivid action, I called long distance information and attempted to get the telephone number of the Ayatollah. Unfortunately, he has an unlisted tent and could not be reached. It was probably just as well because, searching my brain for anything in my last collection that might have the happy effect of giving offense to the Most Worthy One, I could only recall one blurb from a distant column to the effect that everytime I saw him on television I thought it was Gabby Hayes in drag. Realizing deep down that this flip and off-the-cuff observation wouldn't generate an Iranian bounty of more than two or three hundred dollars, I began my quest for a condemnation by some other potentially indignant past victim of my venomous pen.

I called Roger Sund, the Executive Director of the Cobb County Chamber of Commerce, and pointed out that in one essay I had alleged that Cobb County was not as sophisticated as it held itself out to be, going on to report that a group of anthropologists at the University of Georgia had recently discovered a tribe of people living in the woods in South Cobb County who still worship the Big Chicken. I suggested to him that the Cobb Chamber might want to put out a contract on me and offered to kick in a couple of hundred bucks to the fund myself if he could get some radio and TV time to publicize the threat. Sund said that he was not interested in that the Chamber had already relocated all the Big Chicken worshipers in mobile homes near Smyrna, and, "besides," he said, "nobody in Cobb County reads your stuff anyway."

Undaunted, I resumed poring over my prior literary output for other serious slights which could be thumped into a newsworthy public grievance with resulting salutary effects on book sales.

I had observed irreverently in the past that if Ronald Reagan had one more face-lift, his navel was going to pop up over his shirt collar but, on reflection, I decided a death threat from an ex-President would not be sufficiently newsworthy to get a blurb in *Creative Loafing*. I then recalled that I had once publicly suggested that Six Flags Over Georgia install a new thriller and death-defying attraction consisting of an automobile ride with Hosea Williams (talk about your Scream Machine). Remembering that Hosea was pretty volatile, armed to the teeth, I called his office to see if he might utter a threat with respect to my book but through his secretary was given a polite brush-off to the following effect, "Tell that chump I ain't studying him."

If any readers have any suggestions as to how I might have given or could in the future give ultimate offense to some powerful and newsworthy person and provoke a public jehad along the line of the *Satanic Verses* hurrah in the process, I would welcome their suggestions. In the meantime, I am optimistically storing provisions in a secret hiding place (all I can tell you is that it is somwhere in the metro area) against the possibility that I might have to go underground for a spell if I ever come up with the right person to antagonize.

Robert L. Steed

February 20, 1989

March 4, 1989

Mr. Robert Steed
c/o *The Atlanta Constitution*
Atlanta, Georgia

Dear Mr. Steed:

You mourn that you have not insulted anyone badly enough to have someone put a price on your head and thereby increase your book sales.
How about your wife?

With best wishes,

Harry Williams

March 21, 1989

Harry — If she ever read my column, I'd have to hire a food taster. Happily, her lips get tired before she reaches the op-ed page.

April 25, 1989

Mr. Richard Allison
Alston & Bird
Atlanta, Georgia

Dear Alice:

Enclosed are some Frozen Moments in Time for your Golden Book of Memories with the Steeds.

The photos of you, Lamar [Dodd] and the Alston & Bird painting are particularly good, although I wish you had been able to button your coat.

I talked with him yesterday to say how much we enjoyed the visit and his hospitality and how pleased you were to get the watercolor. He said (and I think this is a sign for you to gird your financial loins), "I really hated to part with that one, but the Allisons are so nice." When I told him of your vast landholdings in southwest Alabama, he seemed a good deal less unhappy with his decision to make the sale.

With warmest regards, I remain

Up to My Nether Regions
in Baptist Alligators,

Robert L. Steed

Robert L. Steed

August 29, 1988

Mr. Darrell Fennell
Gould, Cooksey, Fennell,
  Appleby, Barkett & O'Neill
Vero Beach, Florida

Dear Darrell:

I'm doing well, thanks, but have an increasing tendency to "bunch up" when I sit down and get winded with any strenuous physical activity such as changing channels on the television set or moving from one place to another. Lu has shown no improvement since you saw her last, though I have promised the children that we'll keep her with us as long as we can, but she really ought to be in a home somewhere. She and I went to New York for three days last week to celebrate our 30th anniversary and had a great time — saw "Phantom of the Opera" and danced the night away at the Rainbow Room. Though her mind is a little fuzzy, she still has plenty of spring in her step. . . .

Georgia Steed (child No. 2) is getting married on October 15 to a young lawyer in Atlanta whom we like very much, so this fall has been filled with a welter of prenuptial activities. Josh is enjoying real estate work in Atlanta, and Nona is a senior at UGA where she is majoring, I think, in parking tickets and bank overdrafts.

It's good that both of us started our families while

we were still so young, otherwise, we'd be getting old by now.

With warmest regards to you and the Senora, I remain

Cute as a button,

Robert L. Steed

Following an unsuccessful attempt by the North Carolina National Bank to take over the Citizens and Southern Corporation, Steed sent the following message to C&S Chairman, Bennett A. Brown:

April 27, 1989

Mr. Bennett A. Brown
Chairman
The Citizens and Southern Corporation
Atlanta, Georgia

Dear Bennett:

Congratulations on fending off the Bank of Mayberry. You folks did it just right.

I think your response was the banking variation on the always thoroughly effective response — "Not tonight, dear, I've got a headache."

I imagine Brother McColl is taking a cold shower and all of the lawyers are flying their briefs at half-mast.

Best wishes.

Sincerely,

Robert L. Steed

September 21, 1988

Mr. Gil Campbell
Tennessee Bar Association
Nashville, Tennessee

Dear Laddie:

Sinister forces conspire to prevent me from going to the fourth annual Gator-Hater Golf Tourney this November. There, there, buck up. This doesn't mean that you can't go; I have worked out an alternate arrangement with Colonel Parker in your behalf, but more about that later.

Just when I was getting excited about a golf outing with the literary segment of the UGA Alumni Association (yes, "Go Dogs" is a complete sentence), I was informed by Longstreet Press that I had been scheduled for an autograph session at Oxford Book Store for my new book, *The Sass Menagerie*, (incidentally, how many can we put you down for?) on November 4, 1988. I quickly informed them that would not be possible as I planned to be tacking about the Sea Palms Golf Course with Chi Chi Grizzard. To describe their reaction as that of a fire in a whorehouse would be a rank understatement. They began to whimper and cavil, insisting that I *had* to make this appearance lest other *real* authors on the Longstreet list be prejudiced in the eyes of Oxford by my defection. I, of course, ultimately acceded to their pitiful importunings.

I called Joshua Pentecost Steed alerting him of

this development and urging him to go without me. He dutifully declined, which caused my eyes to moisten a bit until Lu pointed out the next day that if he had gone on his own, "he would have to pay all those caddy fares and stuff." The woman may be old but her mind is as clear as a bell.

As I had worked long and hard to secure for you a non-golfing spousal permit to attend the function, agreeing, in your behalf, that you would agree to any "normal" conjugal privileges that might be requested of you by the fee-paying golfers to whom you were assigned (or should I say "attached"), I was apprehensive about approaching Colonel Parker in your behalf now that Josh and I were not planning to attend. As you will see from the enclosed material, he has set a $225 fee for the Tourney in addition to the cost of accommodations (with respect to which he also gets a slice, I suspect). By my calculations, this results in a net profit to Grizzard Enterprises from each participant in the range of $175, and I was afraid he might want you to belly up for the full amount. The fear that I might expose him to those slow-witted Georgia alums he has been bilking for four years has now caused him to agree that your invitation was still open and at the bargain price of $25.

Accordingly, I am sending all of my mailing stuff to you so that you can follow up. I think you can bunk with Mike and David (assuming you have a pair of those Jim Palmer jockey briefs) as I do not believe their spouses are going to make the trip.

Trusting all of my efforts in your behalf in this regard are acceptable to you and leaving you to your own devices and the tender mercies of Colonel Parker, I remain.

A legend under the kilt,

Robert L. Steed

September 27, 1989

Mr. Gil Campbell
Tennessee Bar Association
Nashville, Tennessee

Dear Gil—

You were much missed by the Caledonian Revellers last evening. The outing turned into a complete debauch. Champion [Bob] Dhue wined and dined us in the Omni President's Box and then, for reasons which have fogged over in my memory, we all thought it would be a splendid idea to go to the Gold Club to see Lewis' [Grizzard's] favorite ballerina, the lovely, highly intelligent and very talented Carlotta.

If you haven't ever visited that establishment, you really should go just to round out your education. It is absolutely surreal. I can't begin to describe the full effect except to say that I felt as though I was swimming upstream in a sea of nudity. We did indeed meet and *see* Carlotta, who looked very much like a junior high school student. She seemed very devoted to Lewis but those warm feelings may have been enhanced by the $100 bills that he kept putting in her garter. Mike Steed, seeing this, offered to take off his clothes but we couldn't find a garter big enough to circumnavigate one of his pudgy legs. . . .

With warmest regards, I remain,

Rigid and unyielding,

Robert L. Steed

June 19, 1989

Mr. Tony Privett
Impresario
Grizzard Enterprises, Inc.
Atlanta, Georgia

Dear Colonel:

As I was browsing through my Encyclopedia of Southern Culture (over 1,500 pages) last Friday evening looking for my name, I was absolutely flabbergasted (a condition often caused by fluid retention) to see the entry on Lewis Grizzard.

My literary gag reflex was permanently damaged when I came across the line describing him as "the Faulkner of the common man."

Although this opus is just released, it was about three years out-of-date in terms of Lewis' titles. I was also glad to see that they didn't list *Creative Loafing* as a source.

I was also disappointed that the sketch makes no mention of Lewis' extraordinary talent as a stand-up (and gross-out) storyteller whose impromptu performances at country clubs and restaurants are a growing part of our Southern Tradition.

To learn that Uncle Lewis was big at the Gold Club and in the Encyclopedia of Southern Culture was too much for me.

With warmest regards, I am

Still smarting,

Robert L. Steed

To Mike Steed
from Italy:
(10-15-82)

The trip has been great
but I'm sorry to report
that Lu bought a fur
coat (collie, we think)
off a pushcart yesterday.

Bob

The following is a thank-you note from Steed to his friend, writer Art Harris, who wrote an exposé on Jimmy Swaggart for Penthouse *magazine.*

August 16, 1988

Mr. Art Harris
Chronicler of Concupiscence
Atlanta, Georgia

Dear Art:

Are you any relation to Frank Harris? I suspect your prurient prose has now been read by more folks than his.

Many thanks for your thoughtfulness in remembering my request for an autographed Swaggart *Penthouse*. I will add it to my cache of concupiscent classics which include the Vanessa Williams edition, Madonna unadorned (and looking like the high princess of the "Don't Shave Anything League") and Jackie Onassis sunbathing in the buff on some ancient Greek Island (or maybe it was an island owned by some ancient Greek).

Your gift is especially treasured because I never was able to score one on my own. In the early days after its release I could have bought one but there was always a woman clerk or someone with a coat and tie standing behind me in the convenience store line. I have the same difficulty at movie house concession stands too. I'm always embarrassed to say "Goobers" out loud.

With renewed thanks and warmest wishes, I am

Easily aroused,

Robert L. Steed

Ms. Marianne C. Thomasson
Managing Editor (and conjugal partner
  to the Publisher)
The Newnan Times-Herald
Newnan, Georgia

Dear Sister Marianne:

Thank you for letting me know that Sister Lillie Bell Johnson has "Crossed Over Jordan."

The most sobering aspect of the communique was that Sister Johnson came into this life on February 12, 1935, scarcely a year sooner than I. Moreover, her good works while here far exceed mine. She clearly had many stars in her crown while I am only accumulating dents in my head.

With warmest regards, I am

> Here to help sing a little bass and otherwise assist in the general mourning,
>
> Robert L. Steed

April 26, 1989

Robert Phinizy Timmerman
Aiken, South Carolina

Dear Phinizy:

Enclosed you will find a Commemorative Cartoon from the incomparable pen of David Boyd reflecting our happy outing as your guests on Augusta National.

Brother Mike (whose play, you will recall, was less than stellar) is the one depicted with the bag on his head. On the way back, he was waxing philosophic about the damage he inflicted on the course during his round. He said, "Well, the caddies were carrying around seeds to restore the divots." Boyd said, "Yeah, but they weren't carrying anything to put bark back on the trees."

I hope this note finds you with plenty of spring in your step and a slow, smooth, backswing.

With warmest regards, I am

Looking Up on Every Shot,

Robert L. Steed

June 8, 1989

Mr. Murray A. Galin
Savannah, Georgia

Dear Mr. Galin:

Your wife (I think she had been drinking) called me earlier this week to invite us to be guests in your new Pleasure Dome, and I wanted to accept with alacrity. Unfortunately, alacrity is going to be over in East Alabama at a gospel singing during the time I plan to be in Savannah and, accordingly, I am going to bring my wizened wife instead.

The purpose of this letter is to test whether you will stand behind the invitation. I think a case can be made that your wife has apparent authority in this regard as it is generally known in the Savannah area that both the money and looks in the family are in her name.

Her invitation was open-ended and I wish it had been extended before we had already used up so much of our vacation. However, we do look forward to spending the evening with you on Friday, June 30, and will probably arrive at Casa Galin mid-afternoon if I am successful in tearing myself away from the very important legal matters in which I am typically engaged.

You will be happy to know that for the balance of the weekend, we are booked into Georgia's Golden Isles and thus will be leaving you sometime before noon on Saturday, July 1.

I will be speaking to the South Carolina Bar at noon on the first as they are meeting in Savannah (go figure!). In lieu of a "bread and butter" gift, I would be delighted to see that you and the Rose of Sharon are included as my guests at the luncheon. While most of the material is over your head, she would certainly add a lot of luster to our luncheon roster.

If you don't want to renege on the invitation, please send me directions to your new abode and let me know if we should bring our own linens and towels.

Looking for some white smoke from your hospitality chimney, I remain

Reasonably alert,

Robert L. Steed

July 7, 1989

Mr. and Mrs. Murray A. Galin
Savannah, Georgia

Dear Gala Galins:

My wizened wife and I certainly enjoyed having our feets under your table last week. Your prodigious hospitality warmed the cockles of our heart. (A recent study at Emory University revealed that almost 75% of all patients checked who were over 50 years of age had heart cockles.)

When you called us some weeks back to invite us to stay with you during the Bar convention, Lu remembered Sharon but had forgotten Murray (and who can blame her), so she was delighted to get acquainted. Her exact words were, "I give him an 85. He's cute as a button and can play the harmonica." I think that says it all for both of us. Aside from the marvelous company and splendid hospitality, the carriage ride and crab cakes stand out in my mind's eye. The rug we bought is now a "throw" on the back of a big over-stuffed couch, giving an overall feeling of a waiting room in a Turkish bordello and offering enduring memories of our Savannah Sojourn.

As tangible evidence of the eternal verity of the maxim that "No good deed go unpunished," I am enclosing The Compleat Collected Works of Robert L. Steed. Read sparingly and at random intervals so no permanent damage will be done to your literary gag reflex. Lu Steed is also enclosing a modest "bread-and-butter'' gift which can't hold a candle to my offering. In Lu's defense, Emily Post says you don't have to give too nice a bread-and-butter gift if the butter was frozen.

With warmest regards, I am

Thoroughly sated,

Robert L. Steed

P.S. I called London this morning re: the *Phantom* tickets. They will inquire and call me back.

July 12, 1989

Mr. and Mrs. Murray A. Galin
Savannah, Georgia

Dear Funseekers:

I regret to report that my man in London (I.D.G. Taylor) called me today to say that there were no reasonably priced tickets available for *Phantom of the Opera.* He says the situation is bleak and that bad seats are going for 75 pounds with good seats going for 120 pounds. I enjoyed *Phantom* very much but I agree that there is not that much enjoyment to be squeezed out of it. I would spend the money on important things, like food, clothes and plastic replicas of Big Ben and catch *Phantom* when the Pooler Little Theatre gets around to it.

Keep on the sunny side!
With warmest regards, I am

Increasingly jowly,

Robert L. Steed

October 18, 1989

Rabbi Ben Murray
   and Sister Sharon Galin
Savannah, Georgia

Dear Gala Galins:

You folks went above and beyond the call of friendship with our London friends, the Taylors. Lu and I
send you our warmest thanks for being so very hospi-
table to them. We got a glowing account from them
about your hospitality which made us feel very warm
indeed. The warm feeling was marred slightly by Lu's
observation to the effect that, "Hell, they weren't that
nice to us." I think we all have to make allowances for
Lu.

In any case, the Taylors gave us full credit for
having such gracious friends. If you are that nice to
any friends we send to see you in the future, we may
even send back the towels.

Ian came away convinced that Murray was quite a
celebrity because he said that everywhere they went
everyone knew Murray. I solved that mystery right
away when, after a few questions, I learned that the
only places you went were bars.

With belated thanks and love to you both, we are

Sticking Together for
the Children's Sake,

Robert L. Steed

The following is Steed's reply to a letter from a young friend attending Suwanee who sent some newspaper clippings featuring wedding photos of an unusual looking couple of Tennessee rustics.

February 3, 1989

Mr. R. Byron Attridge, Jr.
University of the South
Sewanee, Tennessee

Dear Nairy Bird:

I appreciate your sending me the clipping with the account of your fraternity brother's wedding at the Wendy's Restaurant in Dechard. I could tell by looking at the photo that he was a SAE, though based on my experience with SAE's at Mercer back in the 50s, I would have been thrown off a bit by the fact that he was getting married. Most of the SAE's I knew in my college days were "light in their loafers" and wore those jockey briefs with the days of the week embroidered on them. The real studs were Phi Delt which, by coincidence, was my lodge.

As for the need for additional seating at the Franklin County Football Stadium, I would urge you to write the *Herald-Chronicle* a letter suggesting that all of those redneck peckerwoods simply sit on their haunches as they have been doing for hundreds of years.

Be good, study hard and stay away from Debbie's Hideaway. Some people have come back from there with a rash that penicillin couldn't begin to dent.

Avuncularly yours,

Robert L. Steed

December 30, 1988

Matthew H. Patton, Esq.
Republican Party Activist
Kilpatrick & Cody
Atlanta, Georgia

Dear Rev. Patton:

I note with interest (and a slight gagging sensation in the region of the epiglottis) that you are quoted
in the *Fulton County Daily Report* as "continuing to
toy with" the idea of entering the 1990 race for President of the State Bar. While I am pleased to note that
you are not still "toying" with the same thing you
were back in your youth, I am dismayed at the thought
of adding yet another mullet to those already contend-
ing for this spot—deMayo and Lester. I think the fact
that two such weak and lackluster candidates have
already offered for the post gives us a black eye in the
eyes of the public and your addition would serve only
to lower the overall quality of the already nadir-like
mix currently in contention.

As that great American philosopher J. D. Hardman once observed to me regarding you, "That fool
wants to be the bride at every wedding and the corpse
at every funeral." I, of course, leapt vigorously to your
defense pointing out that part of your posturing was
just an attempt to overcome the humility suffered at
being fired from a menial job at Southwire some weeks
earlier. But, on reflection, I think Hardman may have
been right. I urge you not to run for State Bar Presi-

dent but, instead, to keep up your splendid endeavors on behalf of the Republican Party. Senator Mattingly was certainly a bright spot in our pantheon of Georgia leaders, and I am one of a growing number of folks who think it's time for a comeback by Roscoe Pickett and Fletcher Thompson. If I can be of any service to you in this regard, please feel free to call on me at any time. Of course, my secretary will answer, but I'll try to get back in touch with you as soon as I can.

With warmest regards to you and all under your protection, I am

Subject to wild mood swings,

Robert L. Steed

Robert L. Steed

September 15, 1988

The Executive Committee
Lawyers Club of Atlanta, Inc.
Atlanta, Georgia

Gentlemen (and such Ladies as may have slipped on
the Committee while I wasn't watching):

This letter is to warmly endorse the candidacy of P.
Russell Hardin for membership in the Lawyers Club.
Russell, a native of Lake Junaluska, North Carolina, is
an undergraduate of the University of Virginia and a
law graduate of Duke University.

For a time he worked as a lawyer at King & Spalding, but, borrowing a felicitous phrase once uttered by
Roscoe Pickett, Esq., he left us and "answered the call
of the coin" to join an investment banking firm. Later,
sensing instinctively that there was even more money
with the various Woodruff Foundations than there was
in the investment banking community, he soon
decamped and is now the number two man (person)
for the management of all of the various Woodruff
charitable interests.

I would say that we could certainly do worse than
adding P. Russell Hardin to our roster, and I urge you
to give his proposal prompt and positive consideration. During your deliberations in this regard, I hope
you will take to heart the thoughtful admonition of our
esteemed member Tom Watson Brown, Esq., who said,
"The more of these suckers we sign up, the better

chance we'll have of keeping the drink prices down at the Club."

With warmest regards, I remain

Loyal to the core,

Robert L. Steed

P.S. There will likely be some who will be contacting you against Mr. Hardin, citing his involvement in various sightings which he reported in the late 1970's of the "Lake Junaluska Monster." I think he has thoroughly explained all of that business admitting that he had "had a couple of beers" and conceding that the sightings could have been "ground fog." In any case, I am confident there was no question of conscious fraud on his part and that he was sincere in his beliefs.

R.L.S.

October 1, 1987

Mr. Tony Privett
Mr. Lewis Grizzard
Grizzard Enterprises, Inc.
Atlanta, Georgia

Gentlemen:

I am almost embarrassed to send you the attached missive knowing full well that you don't need the money. However, just having money isn't always enough as money can get out of your hands. I direct your attention to the paragraph in the enclosure dealing with "special Mojo Hands" that will "make you hold Money when you get your Hands on it . . ."

This letter is my first contact with Prophet Bates (All Seeing Prophet) so, of course, I can't warrant any of the information set forth in his letter. It does seem to me though that $20 and a few hours on Friday evening is a small investment to make for such long odds on potential gain.

Lu and I are going to try to get there as close as possible to 7 P.M. and will hold four seats for your group.

Looking forward to seeing you then, I am

Standing on the promises,

Robert L. Steed

My Dear Christian Friend:

This letter may come as a surprise to you but it is a blessing straight from Heaven because I am on my way back to Atlanta, Georgia, on this Friday night coming for a very very special Healing and Blessing service, and everybody what sees me can Hit the thing dead straight without fail.

I am that great Prophet that people is talking about all over the country because I gives out two and three straight Hits everywhere I go. As you know they call me the (All Seeing Prophet) from Texas and I now Pastor in Baltimore, Maryland, plus I have branch churches in Detroit, Michigan, Chicago, Illinois, and other areas and many people is getting rich off my blessings, so if you need Money in a hurry make sure to see me on this Friday night coming and I double guarantee you that you can Hit the thing dead straight.

I want you to know that I am a man of God and I don't believe in playing with God or trying to fool folk, so I am saying to you right now if what I tell you is not right you can get every dime of your money back or I hope God to Paralyze me stone cold dead.

Everywhere I go people get quick action and fast results to their problems, especially if you have money problems because I always find out what the thing is going to be before I come to town and you can always Hit it straight. In fact, I was down there in Atlanta on last Sunday a week ago and I told all of my followers and their friends who came to see me to read Psalms 10:1 for their money blessing and read it all three ways and it fell like a ton of bricks on last Monday and folk is still shouting, and if you meet me this Friday night coming you can do the very same thing without fail.

Yes, my dear Christian friend, on this Friday night coming October 2, 1987, I will be back in the city of Atlanta, Georgia, for another very special blessed service and I will be conducting service at the Holiday Inn Downtown at I-75 Piedmont at Courtland and I will be in the Grant Hurt Ballroom at 8 P.M. sharp and I want you to know that this will be the greatest blessing and Healing service ever to take place in Atlanta, Georgia.

For the benefit of you and all of my followers and friends I have asked the folk there to have the doors open at 7 P.M. and service will start at 8 P.M. sharp, and if I was you I would come early and get a good seat as I am always crowded whenever I come to town for everybody knows what I can do and it is always dead straight and one-way the day I say.

Along with a straight Hit for money, I am also bringing a generous supply of my special Mojo Hands that will make you hold Money when you get your Hands on it and also special annointing Oils for the sick and afflicted, and once again I say unto you that this is it. You don't have to look no further this is it. I have the straight thing for you that will fall dead straight in one day and you can Hit for all the Money that you want to. Now in case you are wondering where I got your name from, an old follower of mine whom I have hoped a many a times in the past told me about you, and they also said that you needed cash money and could keep your business to your ownself but you may bring a close friend or a loved one that you know needs help if you think you can trust them to keep they business to they ownself because, I am going to upset the city there in Atlanta, Georgia, again when I get there and everybody what sees me can Hit dead straight or as I told you before, you can get every dime of your money back so help me God who is up there in Heaven.

There are a many a Prophets that would charge you a whole bunch of money for this kind of straight advice for one day, but I am only asking that you will bring a love offering of only $20 and after you Hit send me a little Tip.

Now I also want you to know that I am not like a lot of Preachers and so called Prophets who don't do nothing they say and you can't find them after they leave town. I am in my Baltimore office during the week and my telephone is at the top of this letter because I stand behind what I preach and I back up what I say and if you need cash and need it quick, make sure to see me this Friday night coming October 2, 1987 at 8 P.M. sharp. Remember the Ballroom will be open at 7 P.M. and service will start at 8 on the dot and I have it for you dead straight and one way I will also name the day.

Spiritually Yours,

Prophet John C. Bates

September 28, 1971

Rev. Haywood Day
Bowdon Baptist Church
Bowdon, Georgia

Dear Rev. Day:

I have studied and prayed over your request for a
love offering to be applied toward the cost of the Pastor's Color TV Fund.

Midway through my deliberations, I recalled the
words of a well known Mercer ministerial student,
Saul "Suckback" Smedley, on this very subject. You
may recall Smedley first gaining fame as a child gospel
singer. His tenor version of "Justice Called and Mercy
Answered" while accompanying himself on the
esophagus tube still causes the Le Fevre family to
twitch in unrestrained envy. Ordained as a Baptist
minister at the age of 12, Smedley left gospel music to
become a faith healer. Operating as "Oral (if I can feel
'em, I can heal 'em) Smedley," his practice was to
loiter about the square in Valdosta, Georgia, and fall
upon passersby with alacrity (Alacrity, later picked
out of a police line-up, claimed he never heard of
Smedley, but that is another story). He would then
wrench his hapless victim's head in concentric circles
simultaneously shouting "Be Healed!" at the top of his
lungs. A group of local citizens, noting the spectacular
drop in tourism, successfully procured an injunction
and Smedley channeled his energies into evangelism.

With nothing more than an army surplus tent and several hundred funeral home fans, Smedley staged a spectacular revival on the banks of the Flint River, climaxing it by baptizing over 300 people, almost all of them by force. Mercer officials, learning of his triumphs, persuaded him to join its theology department as an instructor in freshman snake handling.

It was during his stay at Tatnall Tech that he happened into the Phi Delta Theta Suite while the fraternity men were watching the Miss Macon Swimsuit Competition on the television. Screeching at the top of his lungs, Smedley produced a red letter Gideon Bible misappropriated from the Fire Proof Motel on the Warner Robins highway and screamed words forever etched in my memory — "JESUS NEVER WATCHED NO TV!" (Since that time, I understand that research on the Dead Sea Scrolls, the Yonan Codex and statements by Billy Graham and Hugh Downs have confirmed this fact.)

I offer Rev. Smedley's statement by way of reply to your request.

Thanking you for your attention, I remain

Yours in George Beverly Shea,

Robert L. Steed

The following is an exchange of letters between Steed and his former Mercer schoolmate, Haywood Day, a Baptist minister. Day was chiding him because of the fact that Steed's wife, a known Methodist, had enrolled Steed, a lukewarm but persistent Baptist, as a member of the Northside Methodist Church in Atlanta without his knowledge or consent.

December 20, 1978

Mr. Robert Steed
Atlanta, Georgia

Dear Mr. Steed,

In a historical research project funded by the Fundamentalist Baptist Conference and Parimutuel Gambling, Inc., I have discovered that you recently passed the Committee for the Establishment of Better Baptists and have been admitted to the Bowdon Baptist Church. I congratulate you on achieving such an impossible accomplishment.

Of course, it is not my contention that joining a Baptist Church is difficult. Jimmy Carter and Lester Maddox have accomplished the same. Only comedians like Flip Wilson seem to meet with difficulty. However, it is unheard of for someone to hold membership in two Baptist Churches at the same time.

Some time ago I wrote to you concerning a vacancy on our rolls and offered to add you to our list. This was accomplished on September 31, 1978. Your subsequent membership at Bowdon, therefore, came as quite a surprise.

Although dual membership by paying members is acceptable to us, we request that you not join any more churches. Furthermore, your checks to us should be designated to the Pastor's Color TV Fund.

Your other pastor,

Haywood Day, AB, BD,
MDiv, DMin, SOB

December 28, 1978

The Right Reverend Haywood Day
Fire Baptized Holiness Second Avenue Baptist Church
Rome, Georgia

Dear Brother Day:

Your letter of December 20, 1978, finds me in a spiritual hiatus. Having become an involuntary member of Northside Methodist Church through the malign and covert effort of a former Bowdon Methodist, I find that I am now reinstated at the Bowdon Baptist Church, and additionally, have been added to your roles at the Fire Baptized. So that I might have comfort and guidance during the fight over my letter, I became an interim member of the North Marietta Vichyssoise Baptist Church. This, as you may know, is a small but enthusiastic sect which believes that beatification can be achieved by prayer, fasting and washing the feet in cold potato soup. I am also a Life Member of the PTL Club because of a clerical error in connection with a check I sent in response to a UHF broadcast of an offer featuring "The All-Time Hits of the Platters."

I tell you all this only to explain why I may be late in meeting the pledge you so thoughtfully made in my behalf to the Pastor's Color TV Fund.

With all this joining I still have never seen my "letter." For all I know it may be like Mohammed's Coffin, i.e., suspended between Heaven and Earth.

Worse yet is the uncertainty of it all. The person who caused me to be a temporary Methodist without my knowledge or consent is fully aware of the fact that she can repeat this feat at will and has told me that if I "mess with her" she will make me a Methodist *again*. She, like the Lord (and the Trojan Women), has the power to "giveth and taketh away." Notwithstanding that threat, I am happy to be a Baptist again but frankly admit to you that I will miss the drinking and dancing.

Yours sincerely,

Robert L. Steed

*To Mike Steed from
Chartres Cathedral,
France: (10-5-78)*

Mike —

Tell Brother Warren if he'll
get my letter moved I'll have
this duplicated in Bowdon
Baptist. The dollar is in
terminal condition and I
may be next. Lu, of course,
is doing as well as any of us
could have hoped for.

Bob

July 25, 1986

Mr. Donnie Lee
Shenandoah, Georgia

Dear Hoss:

Accompanying this letter is a small token of appreciation for your prodigious service in leading the West Georgia Skillet Lickers to yet another peak performance at Casa Steed. The rave notices continue to pour in and several people claim to have been healed from maladies ranging from sciatica, lumbago, quinsy, deranged kidneys, parasites and stiff joints (though I can't, for the life of me, imagine why anyone would want to be cured of the latter). If we had just had time to form a healing line, I think we really could have done some good.

I am sorry I didn't get the enclosed to you in time for your vacation as we have had many requests for signed glossies of you in a swim suit. As to why I chose this particular gift, I saw a sign advertising it as a "no brainer." I don't think I need to elaborate . . . even for you.

With warm good wishes and renewed thanks, I am

Standing by the Promises,

Robert L. Steed

September 8, 1987

Mr. and Mrs. Ted Mayden
New York, New York

Dear Ted and Barbara,

    We all felt a little like Amelia Earhart yesterday when we waved good-bye and crept away in the clouds. However, our Long Island Air flight was mercifully uneventful except for some minor damage to my gag reflex which resulted from reading about 50 pages of *Hollywood Husbands* by Jackie Collins which had been left on my seat. I think that constitutes literary littering.

    You folks are great hosts. We enjoyed the weekend from wire to wire, with the possible exception of being stalled in the subway (which Lu claims to have enjoyed as well). Max Shulman began one of his books with: "Bang! Bang! Bang! Three shots ripped into my groin and I was off on the greatest adventure of my life." That opening had nothing to do with what followed, but he explained that he wanted the book to get off to a lively start. The subway trip certainly accomplished that insofar as our weekend was concerned.

    We love the co-op and your tasteful digs at East Hampton. Some of those places are just *too* vulgar, and I commend you both on your taste and restraint.

    With warmest regards, I remain

Eager to mooch,

Robert L. Steed

May 1, 1990

William Emerson, Esquire
Atlanta, Georgia

Dear Squire Emerson:

As promised, I am enclosing *Hairdo* by Sarah H.
Gilbert. I bought this for Lu who spent many happy
hours working in the Moderne Beauty Shoppe, a
beauty parlor owned by her mother which attracted
split ends from as far as Ranburne, Alabama. Lu, of
course, hasn't had time to read it as she is still trying
to finish *Valley of the Dolls* which she bought when it
came out (or perhaps I should say when it "got out").
However, she's making good progress but I don't think
you need to rush through this book on her account.
    With warmest regards, I remain

Pudgy but proud,

Robert L. Steed

In April of 1988, Steed wrote an essay for the Journal of the Medical Association of Georgia *bemoaning the fact that lawyers were held in such low regard by the public while doctors seemed to be revered. It contained the following line which provoked correspondence between Steed and* Atlanta Constitution *editorial page editor Tom Teepen:*

"As a member of that beleaguered brotherhood at the Bar, I am always confounded as to why it is that in every public opinion poll ever taken, doctors and specifically surgeons are always right up there at the top with scientists, astronauts and Mother Theresa, while lawyers find themselves in a knot at the bottom of the pile with used-car salesmen, carnival geeks, chiropractors and Congressmen. After all, the law was a noble and enduring profession when medicine involved little more than pulverizing frog eggs, lizard spleens and yak antlers and surgery was primarily a sideline practiced by barbers."

April 26, 1988

Mr. Robert L. Steed
King & Spalding
Atlanta, GA

Dear Mr. Steed:

Your gratuitous slander of Greeks in the piece you wrote for the Journal of the Medical Association of Georgia is beneath contempt. It is a base canard. It is so bad it is probably a baritone and tenor canard as well. It marks you off as a person who carries prejudice to such lengths that you are now denigrating people not only on an ethnic basis but because of where they work as well. So what if some Greeks work in carnivals? What is so wrong with "carnival greeks"? (You don't even have the decency to capitalize Greeks, as, I must say, even the Turks do.) Do you think carnival Greeks — excuse me, carnival greeks — are worse than bond-flogging yahoo lawyers? I never saw one of your kind open a restaurant.

I want you to know that I have bought a subscription to the medical journal just so I can cancel it. I have never been so insulted in my life, unless you count the times my parents introduced me to their friends as someone else's child.

You better watch out. Remember, Jesus said a Greek shall inherit the Earth. Then where will you be? Out in the cold without a restaurant. Serves you right.

Sincerely,

Thomas Teepoulos

P.S. I wouldn't go to any more carnivals if I were you.

April 29, 1988

Mr. Tom Teepen
Editor, Editorial Page
The Atlanta Constitution
Atlanta, Georgia

Dear Editor Teepen:
By way of reply I offer the following:

A Parable

Once upon a time a Japanese immigrant went to a
Greek restaurant. It was his habit to go there every
night (the "once upon a time" was thrown in just
because it sounded more like a parable). Every night
he sat at the counter and asked for an order of "flied
lice," and every night the Greek proprietor would
laugh, hoot and holler saying "Flied lice! Flied lice!
You always say 'flied lice!'"

This loutish display greatly infuriated the Japanese diner but he kept his tongue until he could no
longer stand it. He then hired an English tutor and for
three months worked on his pronunciation until
finally his tutor pronounced him ready to confront the
Greek. He went into the restaurant, sat at the counter,
fixed the Greek with a steady eye and said, "Bring me
some fried rice, you fligging gleek."

Moral: Beware of Greeks bearing grits.

With best regards, I am

Increasingly incontinent,

Robert L. Steed

The following is an exchange of letters between Steed and a lawyer friend from Carrollton, Georgia, about a Steed newspaper column on jogging.

March 13, 1978

Mr. Robert L. Steed, Esq.
King & Spalding
Atlanta, Georgia

Dear Bob:

I have just read your recent article in the YLS Newsletter. As a county-class jogger, having competed strongly in the recent Victory to Dashboard Mini-Marathon, sponsored by Kate Goldin and the BOWDON BULLETIN, I feel compelled to elaborate directly on a point raised obliquely by your article.

You apparently suspicion that the jogger is motivated by things other than a mature decision to achieve physical fitness or such amorphous concepts as "runners high." Of course, you touched on one of the most apparent motivations and that is that jogging can serve as a sound treatment for chronic shyness by providing an ice-breaker at cocktail parties. The gaunt look to which you referred or, if that look has not yet been obtained, the much coveted t-shirt worn over the tuxedo shirt, clearly marks you as one caught up in the hobby of jogging. This induces a guilt feeling in the flabby non-jogger, enabling the jogger not only to direct the conversation to his area of expertise, but to dominate the conversation thereafter.

Of course, in my judgment, there are much more substantive, deep-seeded and compelling psychological states that motivate the jogger. Among these are:

1. *Masochism.* Contrary to what most joggers claim, the "runner's high" does not occur during the actual run itself. It is usually associated with a sense of release from pain sometime shortly after termination of the run. Some patients at the West Georgia Regional Mental Hospital in Columbus from Carroll County have experienced the same sensation following beating their head against a brick wall.

2. *Exhibitionism.* There are a few other activities that enable one to give vent to this psychological imperative without causing the individual to run afoul of Section 26-2011(c) of the *Georgia Criminal Code.* The compelling nature of this psychological need in joggers is demonstrated by the fact that, even on days at or near the freezing mark, joggers can be seen unclothed from the waist down, except for his or her skivvy-like jogging shorts and Nike waffle trainers.

3. *Diving Board Syndrome—Deprived Childhood.* In many instances, you will find joggers who were deprived in their childhood years by not having access to a swimming pool diving board and were thereby deprived of the four-year-old pleasure of bouncing upon a diving board and calling to one's mother to "look at me mommy." Those suffering this deprivation now accomplish the same objectives more subtly by the previously referred to gauntness and t-shirts. This

syndrome also explains the compelling drive to collect t-shirts.

4. *Large City Induced Suicidal Territorial Imperative.* This is one of the more complicated but equally compelling neurotic needs fulfilled by jogging. As I personally experienced in 1969, it has been generally determined that human beings are not genetically designed to live in such close contact with fellow members of the species as is required by residing and working in a large town such as Atlanta. Having opted for a life contrary to this genetic requirement, some joggers are compelled to run around a regularly defined and ever enlarging territory in an effort to claim it for their own. Dogs have been known to do this in a somewhat similar fashion. However, to-date, joggers have not adopted all the mannerisms thereof, lest they do run afoul of the above quoted Code Section. This particular condition is so compelling that those suffering from it oft times seek to claim that territory on heavily traveled roads and highways in the face of conflicting claims of other equally compelled individuals driving automobiles and semi-trailer trucks.

Now that you have this insight into the compelling nature and deep-seeded psychological needs that lead these individuals to tell their story, I trust that you can be more understanding of these poor souls.

By the way, you may be interested in the results of the Victory to Dashboard Mini-Marathon. J. Thomas "Frank Shorter" Vance finished first by a wide distance. The finish was even more amazing since Mr. Vance had not trained at all. Knowledgeable track and physical fitness experts, however, especially those having a knowledge of Mr. Vance's predilections, noted that his strong finish may have been occasioned by the fact that he crossed the finish line immediately behind a Schlitz Malt Liquor truck that was clocked at 55 miles per hour on its way to Roopville.

I, of course, was not that disappointed in my fourth place finish, since I feel I could have done better had I not tripped over one of the loose strips that I had sewn on my brogans to make them resemble Adidas jogging shoes.

On behalf of the Victory Jogging Club and in view of your interest in jogging, we would like to invite you to the next annual Mini-Marathon and invite you and your friends to participate. Given the fact that the Schlitz truck may be on the same schedule next year, your challenge to Mr. Vance at the finish line would no doubt be exciting.

Until we jog again, I am,

Yours truly,

Richard G. Tisinger, J.D.
(Jogging Doctor)

March 24, 1978

Mr. Richard G. Tisinger, J.D.
Tisinger, Tisinger & Vance
Lex Villa
Carrollton, Georgia

Dear Dr. Tisinger:

Your letter of March 13, 1978, has been entered as an exhibit to a complaint filed by the American Automobile Association as a class action seeking to restrain loose cattle, unleashed pets and joggers. Their point was that each of the three were in approximate parity as to mental capabilities but they were having a difficult time linking joggers to the other two categories before your letter fell into their hands. Their medical people have long contended that jogging produced this unhappy result by causing an interaction between the brain and the skull not unlike that of a dried bean in a mariachi gourd. Your letter convinces them that they have finally found a subject with a head sufficiently large and a brain sufficiently small so as to permit them to effectively test their thesis. If some people in white coats and calipers suddenly materialize in Lex Villa I trust your reaction will be one of cooperation rather than alarm.

In the meantime, I urge you to jog with caution in the rural areas of West Georgia. Mincing about in three-quarter time in short pants and tennis shoes through areas as roughhewn and unsophisticated as Mount Zion, Plowshare and Burwell might provoke some of the more excitable locals into running you down in their pickup trucks and reenacting the love scene from Deliverance.

With warm regards, I am

Increasingly sedentary,

Robert L. Steed

February 13, 1990

Mr. Tony (Colonel Parker) Privett
Corporate Angler and Vigorish Collector
Grizzard Enterprises, Inc.
Atlanta, Georgia

Dear Colonel:

This missive really should be directed to Uncle Lewis [Grizzard] but, taking into account the fact that sending something to him is like mailing a letter to Santa Claus and that you rigorously screen his mail, I am following the traditional procedure and sending it to your attention.

I want to thank Grizzard Enterprises for sending me the lovely photo of that Frozen-Moment-in-Time featuring Lewis' incomparable golf swing.

Not only is he one of our great funny men, the picture will attest that he has one of the funniest golf swings around. That left arm absolutely broke down like a double-barrel shotgun and the club face is not exactly where the golf books would suggest it ought to be. I showed the photo to a golfer in our office and he asked, "Did he fall down after swinging?"

It made me think that the Handicapped Golfers Association was looking for a new Poster Child. If anyone ever writes a book on killing snakes, this photo would be the perfect cover. All of this is simply to say that I have seen better swings on a condemned playground.

The only saving grace of the photo is the fact that Uncle Lewis is wearing a Mercer Classic golf shirt and we will be contacting you later about a "Colonel Parker side deal" to market the photo to our alumni with a view toward deficit reduction. Of course, you will receive your customary "taste."

In the meantime (and before your entire supply of the photos has been placed in Gold Club garters), I would like to request personally autographed copies of it for myself and those under my direct protection (Joshua P. Steed, Burton Vance and Nona Begonia Steed). I would also warn you not to try to foist off photos that you have signed in Lewis' behalf. While his bankers may not be able to detect your attempt to sign his name, I can tell the difference.

So as not to dull Lewis' creative endeavors by squeezing out his juices for this nonsense, I suggest the following by way of inscriptions:

[for Robert L. Steed] "For the sweet swinging Lawyer Steed, who has always been an inspiration to me."

[for Joshua, Burton and Nona] "For my pal (fill in name of pal)"

I know it goes without saying but dealing as we are here with a University of Georgia graduate, I'm going to say it: the foregoing salutations should be followed with a signature.

If there is anything else you can do for me, please don't hesitate to let me know.

With warmest regards, I am

Rigid and unyielding,

Robert L. Steed

The following is an exchange of correspondence between Steed's persistent pen pal, Barry Newman, and Steed regarding a feature article which appeared in the newspapers about Steed's wife, Atlanta artist Lu Steed.

**STATE HOME FOR THE ARTISTICALLY DYSLEXIC
WEST GEORGIA BRANCH**

1988 1 March,

Dear Robert Steed,

I read with intere$t the article in last Sunday's paper about your home. I read a lot here since things are rather slow. My work as a sculptor has fallen off some since they only allow me blunt instruments and a rubber hammer.

I will admit I'm somewhat confused about your house. It has bridges and a two-story, 45-foot-long galley? Are you sure the crew of the STARSHIP ENTER-POOP didn't dock for some chicken wings and y'all wandered in by mistake? Who is Art and why is he hanging in your kitchen? A critic no doubt. I'll bet you even hung some of those plants.

I had heard a while back a nasty rumor that your wife painted large trucks. But I didn't know she was painting floors too. Really, Sir, even if you lost it all in the market crash she shouldn't be doing that kind of work alone. My mother suffers from sinew and it makes unilateral arm negotiation very painful. And her sleeping in a truck, tsk tsk (your wife, not mom).

I hope soon that the nice people here will let me out of this nice white jacket and give me back my sharp objects. Then I can continue with my artistic endeavors. Doubt if they ever give my matches back after I burned down the latrine.

I have done a good bit of carpenter work as you probably know. So if you want to move out of your "space" into a house, gimme a call.

From My Sand Box to Yours,

Barry Newman

March 3, 1988

Mr. Barry Newman
Whittler in Residence
Buchanan, Georgia

Dear Barry:

Thanks for your dispatch of March 1, 1988. You type pretty good for a rustic. I'm also glad to see you're branching out and making your own envelopes now. That is a dying art in West Georgia.

Lu Steed, the subject of the article about which you wrote, is a West Georgia artist as well. She is proud to be 1/16th Cherokee. (If you could see the rest of her family, you'd understand why.) But even with that minute blood line, she still can't handle drinking and gets sullen and detached after a pop or two. When she's not on the juice, she is a creditable painter — particularly of large trucks. She also does portraits now and then but I do the hands and faces. A picture book demonstrating her limited skills is enclosed for your amusement.

As for her sleeping in a truck, she swore it was a *woman* truck driver. Personally, I haven't seen too many of those and I'm not all that sure they slept in the truck. She still hasn't explained where she got the Gideon Bible.

With warmest regards, I remain

Reasonably alert,

Robert L. Steed

July 13, 1987

Mr. Michael P. Steed
Steed Sales Company
Bowdon, Georgia

Mr. David Boyd
The Print Shop
Newnan, Georgia

Dear Fun Seekers:

As you still haven't gotten your itineraries from The Atlanta Travelers, Inc., regarding our forthcoming trip to Scotland for purposes of golf (I suspect they are quietly checking your references), I am making so bold as to send a photocopy of one for each of you.

I'll send you another communique on the dress code but would advise preliminarily that you should not plan to take any drawstring shorts, denim outfits, Massey Ferguson billed caps or strap undershirts featuring UGA logos or coarse sayings. I have checked on Mike's behalf knowing how he likes to play without a shirt on and—based on my estimate of his weight to height—they have assured me this will be all right if he wears a halter.

Until then, I am

A Legend Under the Kilt,

Robert L. Steed

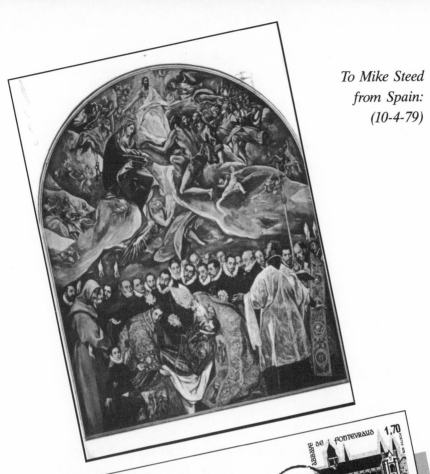

To Mike Steed
from Spain:
(10-4-79)

Dear Mike—

This is El Greco's "Burial of Count Orgaz." Our guidebook says the Count Orgaz (discoverer of the multiple orgasm) died during frantic research. El Greco ("The Greek") got his name by handicapping battles, but he bet heavy on the Visigoths (playing at home) against the Moors and lost his hat, ass and gas mask.

Bob

On August 5, 1987, the Steeds and a group of friends attended a Peter, Paul and Mary concert at Chastain Park in Atlanta. Following the concert, Mary Travers came to the Steeds for a late supper, where the lively and liberal Ms. Travers was confronted by one of Steed's militant and conservative law partners. The following is a subsequent letter to Ms. Travers accompanied by a citation to the obstreperous partner.

August 7, 1987

Ms. Mary Travers
New York, New York

Dear Mary:

Our crowd loved the concert and Lu and I enjoyed having you over for late supper Wednesday evening.

I hope my partner, Lanny ("Rambo") Bridgers, didn't bother you too much with his reactionary rantings. Most of us just carry around a rolled up newspaper and pop him on the nose when he gets out of control. You were, someone has suggested, in a battle of wits with an unarmed man.

Notwithstanding the fact that you took the best two out of three falls, Captain Bridgers' colleagues in the King & Spalding V.F.W. Post saw fit to give him a citation for his Wednesday evening conduct and I thought that you might enjoy a copy. We all agree that

Lanny gave new meaning to the phrase "Blowing In the Wind."

Keep singing and smiling and we hope to see you again sometime soon.

Until then, I remain

Easily aroused,

Robert L. Steed

Robert L. Steed

CITATION

ATTENTION TO ORDERS:

Know all men by these presents that LANNY BOONE BRIDGERS (Captain, United States Marine Corps, Retired, and the pride of Jackson, North Carolina) is hereby awarded the Oliver North Medal of Freedom for distinguished service in defense of human rights and self determination in Central America to wit:

1. On August 5, 1987, Captain Bridgers was lured into an ambush of leftist propaganda at Chastain Park by unscrupulous friends and partners who had misled Captain Bridgers into believing that "Peter, Paul & Mary" was a local plaintiffs' law firm that sang gospel music on the side.

2. The ruse did not last long, however, for almost immediately after consuming his dinner, a third helping of dessert and the remaining two servings of lemon chicken at a neighbor's table, the ever vigilant Captain Bridgers realized that the group "Peter, Paul & Mary" was none other than the folk singing, social activist trip of Peter Yarrow, Paul Stookey and Mary Travers. Captain Bridgers feared that he was in danger of hearing a point of view different from his own and his sensibilities were inflamed. Finally, during a particularly moving rendition of "El Salvador" by the group, Captain Bridgers could contain his red-baiting instincts no longer. Captain Bridgers voiced his displeasure to the thousands gathered at Chastain Park by standing and "booing."

3. Fearing that he had not inflicted sufficient injury to Ms. Travers or the bottle of blush wine that he had just opened, Captain Bridgers declined a tempting invitation to address the Forsyth County Free Speech Society and instead pursued Ms. Travers into the very den of the left-leaning, wrong-thinking, limousine liberal crowd of north Atlanta—a cocktail party hosted by media star and confessed liberal democrat, Bob Steed.

4. Armed with only his acerbic wit, a sweat-soaked madras shirt, white pants and two fists of goose liver pate, Captain Bridgers accosted Ms. Travers about her unabashed socialist sympathies, superficial understanding of complex international issues and the general lack of body and curl in her hair.

5. Ms. Travers was not prepared for the nimble mind, verbal acuity and flawless logic of an accomplished trial lawyer such as Captain Bridgers and was temporarily stunned into silence. She was also distracted by the little drops of saliva that had collected in the corners of Captain Bridgers' mouth during his bug-eyed monologue. She soon recovered, however, and subjected Captain Bridgers to a barrage of facts and figures which has become the calling card of the apologist for Moscow's most recent attempt to occupy Texas. Captain Bridgers did not flinch. When confronted by Ms. Travers' claim that right wing death squads in El Salvador kill over forty people per month, Captain Bridgers coolly retorted, "Did Not!"

6. With total disregard for his own personal safety or the obvious embarrassment of the other guests, Captain Bridgers continued the assault on Ms. Travers until he was finally forced to withdraw from the field because of a particularly effective rear strangle hold that was administered to his head by his lovely, but wiry, wife Linda.

7. Captain Bridgers' attack on August 5, 1987 (that is to say an assault upon an unarmed female in a well-lighted room) is in keeping with the highest traditions of the United States Marine Corps and has brought great credit upon himself and his profession.

Halza Montazuma,
Lieutenant Colonel,
United States Marine Corps

May 14, 1990

Mr. Tom Teepen
Editor, Editorial Page
The Atlanta Constitution
Atlanta, Georgia

Dear Editor Teepen:

I was so flattered by your recent request for some extended filler that I bestirred myself over the week-end to come up with the enclosed bit of froth. I hope you deem it a worthy offering sufficiently bestirred.

Resorting to the *Wall Street Journal* in search of grist for my tiny mill is, I think even you will admit, a *tour de force* [Fr. a forced trip or excursion].

My trusted secretary of many years, Yvonne "No I won't but I'll be glad to give you directions to the coffee room" McMillian, asked, "Was there really an ad in the *Wall Street Journal* like this?" I interrupted my busy schedule to explain to her that we newspaper people can't write something unless it is confirmed by at least two separate sources. I am enclosing a photo-copy of the ad itself and my second source is Captain Walter Strow ("Worts" spelled backwards) who con-firmed the story but asked that our interview be treated as "deep background," whatever that means.

You may wonder at the excessive alliteration in the penultimate paragraph. It is intentional. Recent stud-ies by Masters and Johnson have revealed that a significant number of female newspaper readers actually become aroused at a succession of sibilant sounds. With every good wish, I remain

Gray and drab,

Robert L. Steed

* * *

CALL ME THE Apostle of the Obvious, but I find the *Wall Street Journal* a bit gray and drab (not to be confused with a large Atlanta law firm by the same name). I suspect my impression results in large part by reason of the fact that most of my savings are tied up in a War Bond my grandparents gave me in 1943 while the rest are in a bank Christmas Club account which pays no interest.

Beyond that, the WSJ has no sports section, no funny papers and no TV listings. However, on a rare and random occasion, it can cough up an interesting kernel or two for the alert reader.

Just last week, as I browsed through an abandoned issue in an airport waiting room, I came across an extraordinary advertisement offering "pre-owned watches, including Rolex, Cartier, Patek-Phillipe (which, until then, I had thought was a French milk of magnesia), etc. at prices starting as low as $400."

The ad featured a beefy-looking pilot in front of a propeller-driven airplane who was described as a "captain with a major American airline." The ad went on to say that Captain Strow (obviously not his real name)

"could easily afford a new watch, but he, as thousands before him, opted for the wiser choice . . . PRE-OWNED!" The ad was placed by Grafstein & Co. ("wholesalers to the Trade since 1939") with establishments in Santa Ana, Beverly Hills and New York.

To illustrate just what bargains were available to wrist watch *arrivistes,* the ad featured a photo of a Rolex SS – Gold Datejust which retailed originally for $3,650 but which could be snapped up from Grafstein for a mere $1,790. The ad didn't say what the "SS" stood for but one assumes "Silly Sap," i.e., one who would pay $3,650 in the first place for a wrist watch which had gold pimples instead of numbers.

It is absolutely mind boggling (though some have observed that my mind boggles more easily than most) to imagine a business enterprise dealing in used watches which could afford to advertise in the *Wall Street Journal.*

Come with us now through the magic of a sick imagination to the plush Beverly Hills showroom of Grafstein & Co. as some parvenu seeks to certify his sociability by upgrading his timepiece.

A sales person dressed in a pair of pinstriped pants and a black swallow-tailed coat is cooing to the customer, "This particular Rolex was previously owned by a basketball player who turned professional after only three years of college and thus never learned to tell time. I mean the watch has barely been looked at. It can be yours for a mere $1,790."

Customer (good naturedly): "What's the 'SS' for? Silly Sap?"

Salesperson (haughtily): "Don't be jejune. Besides, that gag was used earlier in the column."

The clear danger (other than a third reference to "SS") is that this trafficking in expensive used watches represents a very dangerous trend. As everyone who has given the matter any serious thought can appreciate, obscenely priced watches have a very important place in our modern society.

Without them some chump sitting next to an important person would not know that he was a chump and the person next to him was an important person unless the important person was able to flaunt a wrist watch costing roughly as much as a new four-door Hyundai. What then will become of the social order if every upstart can appear to be an important person by simply buying a Rolex Oyster *secondhand*?

It's critically important that important people have a clear cut method of declaring their importance and, while alligator attaché cases, Gucci anythings and car phones help, nothing else makes such a supercilious statement so succinctly as a stratospherically priced time piece.

I don't have any answer for all this but it's certainly something for you to think about when you're not heavily engaged in other high-minded and challenging activities, like watching the Newlywed Game or looking through the *Wall Street Journal* for something interesting to read.

Robert L. Steed
May 14, 1990

The following is a thank-you note from Steed to airline pilot John Davis, who sent him a $25 imitation Rolex watch which Davis purchased in New York's Times Square after reading Steed's column on used watches.

June 6, 1990

Captain John Davis
Smyrna, Georgia

Dear John:

What an unexpected dividend from my nonsense on used Rolex watches! I am absolutely flabbergasted (which, taking into account my ever increasing girth, is exactly the right word).

I have been wearing the watch since Gloria presented it to me (in a tasteful but very informal ceremony conducted in my office) and except for a green wrist and a slight port list, have suffered absolutely no side effects.

The great mystery to me is that if the Taiwanese can make these beauties out of old Budweiser cans and package, distribute and sell them for under $25 a unit, why can't they take back the Mainland? You'd think they could get a few wrecked Hondas from a junk yard and make enough ICBMs to bring Dung Chow Ping (spelled phonetically for convenience of secretary) to his knees.

In any event, your thoughtfulness is genuinely appreciated.

With warmest regards, I am

Right on time,

Robert L. Steed

There follows another exchange in the continuing volley between Steed and the militant feminists.

February 8, 1980

Robert Steed
c/o Atlanta Constitution
Atlanta, Georgia

Dear Robert:

I read your article on women and the military.

Because I devote a lot of energy trying to improve the status of women in our community, I will not take the time to respond to all the points you made. However, I want to express my primary objection.

Not only did you degrade all women, but you used the female members of your own family as a vehicle. For this reason I pity them.

In disgust,

Martha Merkin

February 15, 1980

Miss Martha Merkin
Atlanta, Georgia

Dear Miss Merkin:

Have you ever considered the possibility that you are taking yourself too seriously?

Yours sincerely,

Robert L. Steed

March 28, 1980

Ms. E. Lynne Pou
New York, New York

Dear Lynne,

Thanks for the sympathetic note regarding the letter to the editor from the steaming sister. It's good to know that come the Revolution there is some slight hope that one of the bandoleered feminists will hold up her hand to the firing squad and say, "Spare the chubby one . . . he amuses me," or, better yet — "Clean him up and bring him to my tent."

Enclosed is the 8x10 of me for you and/or the prospective groupie who you claim wants to meet me. I must confess that the groupie situation is so desperate that I will sign your friend on without the customary reciprocal photograph and, if she doesn't like the photo (or maybe if she does), I will arrange to come to Los Angeles and appear in person under her pillow at night.

Also, as requested, I am enclosing the reply article, the irate correspondence, which precipitated it, and a letter which appeared smoking in the *Constitution* this morning indicating that the battle rages on . . .

Love,

Bob

Mike —

We are on the way out of
Munich but we had a great
two days at Oktoberfest. The
city is charming and warm
and the food and beer are in
great abundance. My
stomach is on my lap and
stays there even when I get
up. Lu weighs almost 100
pounds without her jewelry.

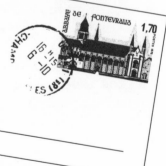

Bob

The following is a thank-you note from Steed to Duross Fitzpatrick, now a United States District Court Judge, and following that correspondence by a few years is another exchange between Steed and Fitzpatrick offering to name Steed as Poet Laureate for the State Bar of Georgia.

August 27, 1982

Mr. Duross Fitzpatrick
Attorney at Law
Cochran, Georgia

Dear Duross:

Thanks for the *Esquire* review of *Hellfire*. I had, in fact, read the book (my brother, Mike, a bluegrass musician by avocation, sent it to me) but I had not seen the review in *Esquire* even though I am a subscriber. The excerpt about Jerry Lee going on before Chuck Berry at the Paramount was absolutely my favorite thing in the book.

The Killer is a bona fide entertainment comet and, like Joplin, Presley, Hank Williams, etc. will burn up before his journey is completed.

My favorite JLL song is "Make Love Sweeter for You"—a little known classic.

The reason I bother to send you these valuable insights in response to your scribbled note is that I fully appreciate how much joy a letter from an important person in Atlanta must mean to someone like you. However, I warn you not to make any attempt to take advantage of my thoughtfulness. I sent a personal note to Brinson one time and he took it all over Rome showing it to everyone who would listen and claimed that he was a "close personal friend of mine." That sorry business finally stopped when he fell on particularly hard times at the end of one month and was forced, I heard, to trade the letter for a haircut. (As an aside, you may be interested to know that Brinson's decline has apparently continued. I learned several weeks ago that he has been admitted for an indefinite period to the Floyd County Home for the Easily Aroused.)

With warm regards to you and my many friends in the Cochran-Bleckley County area, I am

Yours sincerely,

Robert L. Steed

April 16, 1984

Mr. Robert L. Steed
Attorney at Law
Atlanta, Georgia

Dear Bob:

It has occurred to me (and others) that for a great many years you have made a lot of money and gained some notoriety as a lawyer and/or author. You have gained much from your LL.B. but the State Bar has gained precious little from you. I have decided that one of the first orders of my administration as State Bar President would be to appoint a Poet Laureate for the State Bar of Georgia. It seems that this ancient and honorable position has fallen into disuse in recent years. I recall when I was in grade school that the poet laureate of Georgia was Frank L. Stanton who penned those timeless lines:

"Sweetest little baby everybody knows,
don't know what to call him but he's mighty lak a rose."

If you will consent to be our first poet laureate I will see that you get a proper certificate suitable for framing and will give you time at the Thursday luncheon in Savannah (next year) to read your collective works — preferably at the Crystal Beer Parlor.

Somebody told me that Randall Evans had been poet laureate but I suspect that he was only de facto; I want to make you de jure.

Possibly you could collaborate with Chuck Driebe and Jerry Lee Lewis or some other such characters and write us an official song to be sung at the close of every Board of Governors meeting.

Will await your reply anxiously.

Yours very truly,

Duross Fitzpatrick

May 9, 1984

Hon. Duross Fitzpatrick
Notary Public
Cochran, Georgia

Dear Duross:

Please forgive my delay in replying to your letter of April 16, 1984. It reached my office while I was out of town and, as is her custom, my trusted secretary, Yvonne "that file's been lost for years" McMillian, had sorted all of my mail into four customary piles. The "top priority" pile includes new bond issues, good notices about my book, admiring letters, checks of any sort and lingerie catalogs.

The second stack, which we call "high priority," contains business correspondence, intra-firm memos which may affect me in a financial way, buy and sell tickets from my broker indicating his prodigious churning activity in my HR-10 account, and letters from children at various colleges making demands for money.

In the third stack — "low priority" — we have invitations from real estate developers to participate in joint ventures, limited partnerships, tax shelters and the like, catalogs featuring remaindered books from various publishers, requests for charitable contributions, Publisher's Sweepstakes bulletins and alerts, speaking invitations from Rotary Clubs in every Middlesex Village and Farm, and finally, a fourth towering stack (the "flotsam and jetsam" pile) containing mail from the American Bar, State Bar, Lawyers Club of Atlanta, Old War Horse Lawyers Club, Atlanta Bar Association, Georgia Bar Foundation, Gate City Bar Association and the multiplicitous Sections, Committees, Foundations, publications, etc. thrown off by the litter of all of these dubious entities together with myriad invitations to Bar seminars on topics ranging from water and sewer financing under TEFRA to the Uniform Pederasty Act.

Because your kind offer to name me poet laureate, which clearly should have been placed in pile number one, came on State Bar letterhead, it was unceremoniously and thoughtlessly consigned to pile four.

I accept with uncharacteristic humility your kind offer but predict it will result in more controversy than the involuntary separation of my esteemed law partner, George "I'll take no pension before its time" Busbee.

We will likely have to confront the sentiment so lyrically expressed by Pope (Alexander, not McIntire) in his "Essay on Criticism":

"Some have at first for poets passed,
    Turn critics next and proved plain fools at last.
Some can neither for poets nor critics pass,
    As heavy mule is neither horse nor ass."

I have not sent copies of this correspondence to any in the gaggle of disinterested bystanders noted at the bottom of your letter. There are several reasons for this. First, our firm is cracking down on the use of the postage meter for personal correspondence. Second, I didn't know most of them (we couldn't even find Richard Y. "Bradlwy" in the Bar Directory). Third, those whose names I did recognize would not be interested in the question of a poet laureate, having resolved, I am sure, that modern American poetry ended with the death of Ollie Reeves. I did note an interesting juxtaposition of names in "Mr. Henry Crisp" and "Mr. Pat Rice." It occurred to me that if they joined forces with Reginald Eaves they could practice under the name of "Rice, Crisp, Eaves." (It might be observed that Reginald Eaves is not a lawyer but that certainly never held Henry Crisp back.)

You are going to be a great President of the State Bar of Georgia and, God knows, it's time we had one.

Yours sincerely,

Robert L. Steed

One of Steed's closest friends is New York lawyer Barbara Mendel, a militant feminist with a sense of humor sufficiently large to permit her to ignore Steed's perpetual baiting of the feminists.

May 21, 1979

Ms. Barbara Mendel
New York, New York

Dear Barbara:

Charlie Battle and I are delighted to see that the ABA Committee on Legal Status of Women is, in their own words, "flourishing." We noted with interest a Committee which would make even Bill Ide twitch in unrestrained envy. I speak of course of the Subcommittee on Battered Women. We have visions of naked nubile females being dipped in flour, milk and eggs (I have to admit that my fantasies are even more vivid than Charlie's).

The publication "What to do if your Husband or Boyfriend Beats You" must have been inspired by National Lampoon. We want several copies. We thought Ms. Rideout had the answer—sue the Bastard! Our suggestion would be no more dates with the boyfriend ("I've got to wash my hair, dress my wounds, set my leg . . . etc.") and substituting ground glass for hamburger helper in the case of the husband. We suggest that this publication be followed with a monograph on "How Far Can You Go and Still Withdraw Consent?"

In sum, we think your Committee is doing terrific work, and in terms of minority representation you couldn't do better than a Chairperson named Hoy. She might want to consider abandoning the Newsletter in favor of wall posters.

It was great seeing you in New York; don't wear those socks to work.

Love,

Bob

Steed's friend, Bob Young, sent him this news photo of Ronald Reagan and Elizabeth Taylor, asking for a caption. Steed sent several:

• "We plan to call it 'Wean Cuisine.'" —
• "How do you like these Sandinistas?" —
• "What Eddie was really singing was, 'Oh, mein Ta Tas.'" —
• "They were Mike's inspiration for 'The Greatest Show on Earth.'" —
• "I'm a supply sider, too!"

August 24, 1982

Mr. W. T. Moody, III
Executive Director
Macon-Bibb County Industrial Authority
Macon, Georgia

Dear Tom:

Lu will be delighted that you have come forward in her behalf in such a spirited fashion and, while your gallantry is commendable, it must give way to the hard, cruel facts.

Only those people who know her family and their humble circumstances can truly appreciate how far I have brought her in spite of palpable cultural and (even more severe) genetic shortcomings.

Worst of all, she fails to understand, appreciate or acknowledge what I have done for her and persists in chronic and insensitive demonstrations of that fact, to wit: At the Capital City Club pool last Sunday a comely young mother came up to us and said how much she enjoyed my columns. She then said to Lu, "I think your husband is *so* funny," to which Lu replied, "If you think he's funny now, you ought to see him without his clothes on."

Nobody knows the trouble I see.

Yours sincerely,

Robert L. Steed

Robert L. Steed

The law firm in which Steed practices opened a Washington office, which, much to their chagrin and the anger of firm chairman Griffin B. Bell, turned out to be located over a fast food outlet specializing in garlic-laden hero sandwiches. The following is a memo from Steed to the Washington office.

April 23, 1982

MEMORANDUM TO: Mr. John Hopkins
Mr. George Branch
c/o Washington Office

Gentlemen —

Hardly a week passes that our Intrepid Leader does not adjure us to "think of something you can do for the Washington office."

This morning during the firm meeting I thought it would be well if the Washington Office had its own Credo and the following is a very hurried first draft attempt in that direction:

"Send me your rich, your litigious, your politically bereft and deprived, your adulterators of food and drink;

Send me too your cunning realtors, your disingenuous landlords, your investigative office administrative partners and your outraged management committee chairmen;

Send these, the querulous, quarrelsome, fractious souls to me;

I lift my weiner beside the Golden Door."

It obviously needs some work (particularly because of the ambiguous imagery evoked by the closing line), but I wanted you to know that you were in my thoughts and, if matters continue on their current course, my prayers as well.

Robert L. Steed

Political writer Rick Allen took a year's leave of absence from the Atlanta Constitution *to circumnavigate the globe. He sent virtually illegible dispatches to friends, and this is Steed's response to one of them.*

March 8, 1983

Hon. Frederick O. M. Allen
c/o Phineas Fogg Society
England

Dear Ricardo:

I am always pleased to get the dispatches from the ever-shifting "Rick's Place" and number VI was thoroughly entertaining albeit a bit pedantic (*I* know that "Magdalen" College is pronounced "Maudlin." As Homer—the mandolin player, not the poet—once said of Jethro, "He knows a lot of things, he just can't think of them.")

You must be enjoying the UK newspaper accounts of the Americans reeling in the wake of Queen Elizabeth's visit here. It's stirred up some pretty good stuff in the New World as well. Lewis Grizzard had a very lively piece on it making three good points: (1) He said, taking into account the age and appearance of the Queen Mother, she ought to be damn glad to have Jimmy Carter kiss her on the mouth; (2) Of the Queen's complaint that the Mayor of San Diego touched her, Grizzard said we would make a deal whereby we would not touch Queen Elizabeth if Prince Andrew would quit touching porno movie stars; and (3) He said he thought Queen Elizabeth ought to give the Cisco Kid his hat back. The only insight I could have added would be my observation that with all the royal revulsion to kissing and touching, it's no wonder that Prince Charles walks so funny . . .

I had a very lively visit with Ferrol Sams, who was our brunch guest Sunday. Mercer University Press asked him to write a "blurb" for the dust jacket of my collection of columns, and he indicated he would like to meet the Great Author in person. I, of course, leaped at the chance and invited him to dine at Casa Steed. He is a most engaging fellow (a physician from Fayetteville). His wife, also a doctor, is a handsome, slender dark lady who appears to be quite a force in the family unit. He contributed a generous word of praise for the dust jacket (which now includes perjury suborned from the luminous likes of Griffin Bell, Hal Gulliver, Bill Emerson, William Price Fox, Fran Tarkenton, Ali McGraw, Lewis Grizzard and Pat Conroy) and sealed our friendship by commissioning two large paintings by Lu Steed. This caused the grumbling about having to prepare a brunch on an otherwise busy weekend to subside almost immediately. If you haven't read *Run With the Horsemen*, you ought to.

Well, with travel and indolence having an ever-flattening effect on your learning curve, I think I've given you about as much as you can absorb in one sitting and, taking into account your latest literary interest, leave you with the immortal words of Juan Peron — "Doesn't she look natural?"

Yours sincerely,

Robert L. Steed

P.S. Have you ever considered using this slack time to take a course in typing?

June 1, 1984

Edgar H. Wilson, Esq.
Walter F. George
  School of Law
Mercer University
Macon, Georgia

Dear Ed:

Thanks for your note from Kamikaze, Japan. I
don't get that much international mail and was excited
notwithstanding the fact that (1) it came in a Holiday
Inn envelope and (2) contained the disappointing
news that most of the people you talked to had never
heard of me.

Your revelation that you and Carol were the only
Georgians in Japan not travelling at the expense of
YKK also provoked some bitterness on my part. Buckner Melton, who I would not believe under oath or
otherwise, has been blowing cigar smoke up my nether
regions for years about how he is going to take Lu and
me to Japan on one of these YKK boondoggles. He ends
virtually every communication with such a promise. It
has been repeated so often and with such enthusiasm
that from time to time, usually while I am in the grip
of an amber haze, I begin to think that it might be a
possibility.

Earlier this week I talked to George Busbee who
had just returned from Japan (at YKK expense) and
he, unaware of Melton's extravagant and long standing
promises to me, revealed that *one thousand* Americans

were brought to Japan for this recent enterprise at YKK expense.

My immediate reaction was to call Melton and rail at him on the theory that if I ever had a chance of slipping into that flim flam, what better time could there be than to ride in on a 1,000 capacity Trojan Horse. He was, as usual, his glib, expansive and assuring self and, after a good deal more smoke, I was reconvinced of his good intentions and the possibilities of such a trip. Your letter only served to shock me back to reality where I will likely remain until my next visit with that Baron of Bluster, Buckner Melton.

Welcome home.

Yours sincerely,

Robert L. Steed

The following is a letter from Steed to his companions on a fund-raising trip to Japan on behalf of Mercer University.

June 15, 1988

Dr. R. Kirby Godsey
President
Mercer University
Macon, Georgia

Mr. Buckner Melton
Sell & Melton
Macon, Georgia

Dear Kirbysan and Buckysan:

The current edition of *Penthouse* has some shocking photographic evidence of Rev. Swaggart's indiscretions in New Orleans. In the same vein, I enclose for your respective safety deposit boxes some recent photos hot off the press.

The negatives can be obtained for a price, but you should know that [Baptist Fundamentalist] Lee Roberts will be bidding on the other side.

With warm regards, I remain

Yours in sushi,

Robert L. Steed

February 28, 1985

Mr. Daniel R. White
Washington, D. C.

Re: *White's Law Dictionary*

Dear Dan:

Sorry to be late getting back to you on the proofs for your *Dictionary*. I wanted to read it all the way through before replying.

I have done so and judge it to be a palpable hit and would be pleased to be "acknowledged."

I offer the following nits and droppings:

(1) Under "Arguendo" I would suggest that if you want to go for a cheap laugh (and who doesn't?), you might add the following sentence—"Sometimes confused with 'innuendo,' a popular Italian suppository."

(2) I liked the definition of "paralegal" but thought it would have more punch if it were to read, "A legal secretary who can't type."

(3) I offer for your consideration these additional definitions:

(a) *Melvin Belli*—1. A prominent U.S. trial attorney. 2. Latin for "Meet me in Bophal."

(b) *Lexis*—A machine which can do everything an associate can do without criticizing partners or demanding pay increases.

(c) *Euthanasia*—A system of early retirement for senior partners often urged by younger members of a firm.

(d) *Oxymoron*—this might be a better place to lump all of your classic oxymorons and some others, e.g., "Justice Rehnquist," "legal ethics," "lady lawyer," etc.

(e) *Dershowitz*—A Yiddish expression to describe any intellectually arrogant law professor who has a compulsion for gratuitous public expression on almost any subject.

(f) *Per Curiam*—Latin for "none of us wants to take the blame."

With these gratuitous and ill-timed suggestions, I rest my case.

I do indeed remember the lanky Miss Waller. Give her my best (which, these days, isn't all that much).

I have just sent in a new collection of columns for publication this fall. Jack Davis has agreed to furnish the illustrations again, and it's fun pulling this nonsense together. Have you gone back to your day job or are you into this lunacy full time?

Chronically yours,

Robert L. Steed

our room

THE GUANAJUATO REDUCTION & MINES CO.

Guanajuato [Mexico] is even
more lovely than the
guidebooks proclaim! When the
smog isn't too bad from the
mines, we can see the
Reduction Company from our
room. They are busy reducing
my money into smaller
denominations with the
enthusiastic assistance of
Señora Steed, who, despite her
advanced years, has lost none
of her nimble ways with a peso.

The following is an exchange of letters between Steed and a lawyer friend in Tampa, Florida, discussing senior citizen drivers.

March 29, 1985

Robert L. Steed
King & Spalding
Atlanta, GA

Dear Bob:

I just received your most recent column and couldn't resist writing you. No study of driving habits could possibly be complete without at least one section devoted to that segment of the population that one of my law partners refers to as the "wrinkles," but also (less affectionately) referred to as the "old farts." To gather material for this chapter, I highly recommend that you spend 24 hours on the streets of St. Petersburg, Florida. I would recommend a longer period of time than that for full exposure, but that is about as long as one can expect to drive in St. Petersburg without having at least one automobile accident. I note that, amongst the wrinkles, there do not appear to be any distinctions between men and women. Thus, I can only assume that it is a function of age that causes these drivers to progress slowly down the road (approximate speed 20 mph) without regard to (1) traffic lanes, (2) traffic lights, (3) traffic signals, (4) other vehicles, or (5) pedestrians. (This list provides examples only, and is not intended to be exhaustive.) . . .

Very truly yours,

Frances Makemie Toole

April 3, 1985

Ms. Kem Toole
Bush, Ross, Gardner,
  Warren & Rudy
Tampa, Florida

Dear Kem:

Thanks for your note of March 29. I am familiar with the shriveled section of the population to which you refer. Having honeymooned in St. Petersburg some 26 years ago, I still have strong recollection of those wobbly taxpayers. We used to call them "mouth breathers" and, as you know, they still motor through Atlanta in slow moving flocks. They all wear long-billed caps and travel in big cars or recreational vehicles which have signs on the spare tire reading "The Smiths from Ohio." This always makes me want to approach them at a filling station and say "Not *the* Smiths of Ohio."

To save you a step, I am enclosing a paperback copy of *Lucid Intervals* for your friend in Boston. Please send me your marker for $5 made payable to Mercer University. Ruth once told a gathering that the check to Mercer was tax deductible in that they had obtained a ruling from the Internal Revenue Service that the book itself was completely worthless. She went on to say that it was the only time in history the IRS had issued a ruling by return mail.

Ruth is well, as is Frances Ann Estes, although she continues to wear her prosthetic hose. I have always suspected that it is a ruse to put off men who would otherwise be so tantalized by her raw sexuality that they would whimper aloud and think unspeakable thoughts.

By the way, have you considered having them spell out your middle name in the firm letterhead? I think it would get you some business from Hawaii or an obscene phone call or two.

With best regards, I am

Yours sincerely,

Robert L. Steed

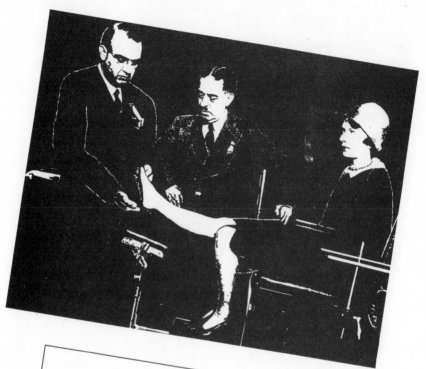

"Yes, Dr. Birnbusch, you're right. It's clearly a case of 'Estes Syndrome.'"

"I would prescribe an ugly elastic stocking with a seam and absolutely no sexual activity until this mess clears up."

From "Feet Don't Fail Me Now" by Dr. Myron J. Lipschutz, Director of the East Bayonne Clinic of Sexually Transmitted Foot Disorders

The following is a speaking invitation to Steed and his reply.

October 30, 1990

Bob Steed
Atlanta, Georgia

Dear Bob:

I would like to invite you to speak at The Third Annual Former Saint Valentine's Symposium before The Obstetrical and Gynecological Society of Atlanta on February 15, 1991. Your spot on the program would be entitled as follows: "Keeping Your Wife Thin and Satisfied While Pursuing a Busy Professional Career."

You will be following Dr. Timothy Fliweight who will be discussing "The Anatomy, Physiology and Surgery of the G-spot." He will be covering such interesting topics as augmentation and reduction of the G-spot according to the medical indications. Following you on the program will be Dr. Leonard Heresay. He will discuss "Pelvic Relaxation: Is It Good or Is It Bad and Can Something Be Done About It?" This talented gynecologist/psychiatrist has traveled the South gathering data on this extremely important issue which affects forty percent of women in the region due to dietary deficiencies. Black-eyed peas, as you know, have been found to be deficient in zinc and other minerals due to heavy clay content of the soil. Concluding the event will be a panel discussion on the topic, "Gynecologist's Apprentice, A New Career Emerges."

Your remarks would be shared with a group of highly skilled obstetrician gynecologists, one third of whom will have male spouses rather than the female variety. This segment will challenge you to bring to bear all of the talents you can muster since house husbands are an increasingly irascible and militant group. They were recently prominently featured in the rear of the room of the Souter hearings.

Thank you very much for your consideration of our request.

Best regards,

Joe B. Massey, M.D., F.A.C.O.G.

November 8, 1990

Joe B. Massey, M.D., F.A.C.O.G., W.I.M.P.
Atlanta, Georgia

Dear Joe:

I would have replied earlier to your nice letter of October 30 but have spent over a week trying to decode "F.A.C.O.G." I finally sent it to our cryptographic unit and they're still working on it. They say they believe the "F.A." stands for "Fecundity Assistance" but haven't come up with anything more.

I would pay to hear Dr. Heresay. Also, I am familiar with spouses. I say they are just like wives except they only shave above the neck.

My speaking agent tells me I'm booked for February 15 but haven't yet received a firm confirmation. (Lack of firm confirmations, as you know better than anyone, is one of the country's leading causes of infertility.)

I will have her (Yvonne McMillian, unlicensed speaking agent) call you next week to see if your date is set in stone.

With warmest regards, I am

Increasingly jowly,

Robert L. Steed

January 7, 1983

Ronald E. Goldstein, DDS
"Dentist to the Stars"
Goldstein, Goldstein & Feinman
Atlanta, Georgia

Dear Ron:

Many thanks for your nice letter of December 6. It's good to hear from someone who enjoys the column as I often hear from those who don't.

In case you missed it, I am sending you an old column which is lovingly dedicated to my dentist, Dr. Solomon "Thumbs" Cohen who goes to dental seminars in Las Vegas; believes that everyone has a colored aura around their head which, in some manner I have been unable to comprehend, affects their dental hygiene; and will pierce yours ears free if you allow him to do an engraving of his choice on the outside of any crown he installs. Some of the subjects he has chosen for my ersatz plastic molars include Golda Meir, Mary Baker Eddy and Sir Philip Phlegm (who, according to Dr. Cohen, invented that little vacuum cleaner they put under your tongue). My bridge is beginning to look like Mt. Rushmore. Not only that, I suspect he has been showing my X-rays to complete strangers but I haven't been able to get any proof.

I don't know how loyal a patient Brother Hal Gulliver is, but he must be working in your behalf on commission. He visited our offices yesterday and gave a thirty minute harangue on your behalf to my law partner, Ruth Garrett. She, acting on the premise that one can become a celebrity by going to a celebrity dentist, finally got Gulliver to go away by agreeing to make an appointment with you to see her much neglected teeth. If she neglects them any further she may well be able to avoid an office visit by simply sending them to you by mail.

I'll close with two questions: (1) Who is the extra Goldstein in the firm name? If it is simply a ruse on your part to enable you to take out twice as much as Feinman, I think he needs a good lawyer; (2) How do you keep Gulliver's Vitalis-laden head from slipping out of the headrest?

Yours sincerely,

Robert L. Steed

July 20, 1983

Ms. Barbara Mendel
New York, New York

Dear Babs:

Enclosed is an excerpt from my new publication—
On the Lamm—which I hope will meet your needs. As
a matter of fact, I think that would be a marvelous
epitaph for me—"He met Barbara Mendel's needs."

Yours sincerely,

Robert L. Steed

September 20, 1977

Mr. W. Stell Huie
Kutak Rock & Huie
Atlanta, Georgia

Dear Stell:

Thank you for the August announcement of the Washington office. It was one of the most complicated ones I ever read and I assume there will be pocket parts.

From a public relations standpoint, I think you missed a bet not leaving the name Yingling & Shay. There are not that many Chinese/Irish law firms in Washington and "Kutak Rock" always sounded like a Polish ginger ale to me.

Everyone has been asking why you had to go all the way to Omaha to find a firm to merge with, and my explanation is that all the lawyers between here and Nebraska already knew about Ide. The surprise is that you didn't have to go to Manitoba.

With every good wish for continued conglomerate success, I am

Yours sincerely,

Robert L. Steed

Robert L. Steed

March 29, 1978

Mr. R. William Ide, III
Kutak, Rock & Huie
Atlanta, Georgia

Dear William:

I appreciate very much the individual announcement of your intergalactic merger and would have been
even more touched if copies had not also been placed in
the windshields of every other car in our parking lot.

You can count on my continued support to bolster
your ever widening practice. I hope plans for the Jesup
office materialize as I know that Roscoe Dean would
like to send the announcements out with his
Christmas cards this year.

Finally, I congratulate you on your national notoriety as evidenced by the following overheard on the
Johnny Carson show just last week:

Karnack: "The answer is 'Kutak Rock.'"
"The question is 'Where did the Polish Pilgrims
first land?'"

With warm regards, I am

Yours sincerely,

Robert L. Steed

Note left in the New York apartment of Barbara Mendel Mayden:

Barbara — The last time I saw an apartment in this condition there were police photographers and a chalk outline of the victim's body on the floor. This makes five consecutive times I've missed you: maybe you ought to sublet this joint and just stay in hotels on those occasions you're in town.

Love, Bob

The following is a thank-you note to lawyer Bill Barwick, who wrote a favorable review of one of Steed's collections, Lucid Intervals, *in the* American Bar Association Journal.

November 25, 1985

Dear Lawyer Barwick,

I liked the review in the *ABA Journal* (it's always good to be mentioned in the same breath with Scrooge McDuck).

I've been watching you for a good while and I now think you're ready for the big time—a letter to *Penthouse* magazine. I have attempted a few myself but everytime I get about half way through one, I get to breathing so heavy that I have to lie down.

My brother in Bowdon got hooked reading those things and we had to have him put in the Georgia Baptist Home for the Easily Aroused in Tifton. He's out now, but for a while there he couldn't even lick a stamp without getting keyed up.

Thanks for gilding the kudzu.

Sincerely,

Robert L. Steed

February 13, 1991

Ms. Karen Vance
Carrollton, Georgia

Dear Sweet Thing:

This will confirm our outing for Saturday, March
2. I have booked a table for six at La Grotta (which is
Italian for "The Grotta").

I would suggest that you and the Tisingers come to
Casa Steed around 7:30 p.m. and we will give you some
drinks that will blur your vision and make us more
interesting or, in Lu's case, not "more" interesting,
just interesting.

I must warn you in advance that she has determined she is 1/16th Indian and has been boring everyone within hearing range to death on this particular
subject. Her problem was exacerbated by "Dances with
Wolves" and by the discovery that if she could docu-
ment her lineage, she would be eligible for some sort of
federal stipend and space on a reservation. She has
visions of going native in her later years on Turkey
Heaven Mountain in Cleburne County. My old professor, Ben Griffith, and his wife, Betty, came from
Carrollton to have dinner with us some evenings back,
and by the time Lu got through bending their ears on
the Indian Question, they were hanging on the drapes
with foam on their withers. I'll do my best to steer the
conversation away from this topic, but forewarned is
forearmed.

I hope this won't sound patronizing but Lawyers Vance and Tisinger should be warned that La Grotta requires a coat and tie and a valid credit card. Those little lawyer outfits they bought from The Hub On The Square, while badly out of style, will probably pass muster.

Until then, I remain

Reasonably alert,

Robert L. Steed

August 8, 1990

Daniel R. White, Esq.
Washington, D.C.

Dear Dan:

Thanks for the latest from Catbird Press, *The Handbook of Law Firm Mismanagement.* Kanter has his finger right on the erratic pulse of law firm administration. I guess there is a great universality in the administrative bumbling that abounds in law firm management. It may be worse in the corporate world. Dave Barry says that corporations hold a lot of meetings because corporations can't masturbate.

You will probably be seeing my name in the news soon as I am about to write a column revealing that Judge Souter is against abortion except in cases of incest, rape and marriage between Andrew Dice Clay and Roseanne Barr.

With renewed thanks and warmest regards, I am

Increasingly incontinent,

Robert L. Steed

Robert L. Steed

February 17, 1989

Mr. Tom Teepen
Editor, Editoral Page
The Atlanta Constitution
Atlanta, Georgia

Dear Editor Teepen:

For circumstances I am unable to explain, I
attended a Hank Williams, Jr., concert last Saturday
evening and a Bon Jovi concert on Wednesday evening.
As I have previously memorialized for the World of
Letters my impressions of Bocephus, I feel it only fair
to do the same for the fast rising Bon Jovi, and the
enclosed effort is an attempt in that direction.

As far as I can tell, the Bon Jovi concert went
unreported in the pages of our newspaper. Perhaps
regular reviewer Bo Emerson is unwilling to risk his
auditory system now that he is a married man with
family responsibilities. As for me, I say it's a noisy job
but somebody has to do it.

With that I leave you to your own devices and hope
that the batteries are fresh.

Anxiously yours,

Robert L. Steed

EVER THE UNWITTING and bumbling victim of cruel circumstances, I found myself last Wednesday evening at the Omni in a boiling mass of barely post-pubescents attending a raucous concert performed by the oddly named Bon Jovi. An unhappy combination of gullibility and inattentiveness always causes me to be the constant dupe of my wiry wife's mercurial musical tastes.

In fact, through lack of attention on my part to her capricious planning and invitation accepting, I had gone from Scylla to Charybdis in the Omni in a span of just four days, having been a casualty of a Hank Williams, Jr., concert on Saturday and the Bon Jovi musical mayhem the following Wednesday.

Correctly judging that reflections on "Why me Lord?" would not help me get through the musical ordeal which lay ahead, I busied myself comparing the crowd in which we had found ourselves engulfed the previous Saturday evening with Wednesday evening's wall-to-wall gaggle.

The contrast was startling. The crowd at the Hank Williams, Jr., concert looked like a casting call for the love scene from *Deliverance.* They were a flint-eyed, beefy and grizzled herd bedecked in camouflage outfits and Confederate memorabilia. The Bon Jovi afi-cionados, on the other hand, were an appealing, very young, well scrubbed lot heavy into miniskirts which looked to have been applied with paintbrushes or jeans which were so amply stuffed they looked as though they had been jumped into from a high place. Their general appearance was remarkably attractive save only the occasional young male whose ear lamentably

Robert L. Steed

sported an earring. I longed to point out to each of them that Willie Nelson never had a hit record after he had his ears pierced but sensed that my message would fall on deaf lobes.

Except for two suspicious looking taxpayers in their 40's with fedoras, shades and dark suits who were apparently doing a bad "Blues Brothers" impression, I was the only grey-haired, necktied music lover in the place. In fact, as I came through the turnstile, a middle-aged ticket taker cracked at me, "You heard Guy Lombardo was dead, didn't you, Bud? It was in all the papers."

As is always the case, we were treated to a warm-up act which, in this case, consisted of four anorexic and gratuitously bellicose teenagers aptly named Skid Row. Their routine, which looked like the Bataan Death March set to music, featured an endless amount of incomprehensible caterwauling.

They all wore tattered bluejeans and shoulder length hair and looked like the children that Don Knotts refuses to discuss. Their upper arms were so spider-like that the tattoos affected by some of them could only have been accomplished with microscopes.

Between their mind-numbing musical selections, they offered in language so foul that it would make Richard Pryor blanch, a philosophy for teenagers roughly as follows: "If like your boss, or your parents, like, or your teacher, like gets on your case and tells you what to do, well then, like, just tell them to go (expletive phrase suggesting an anatomically impossible act deleted) themselves. Because, like, man, that's what rock 'n roll is all about." "Well," I huffed to

166

my zoned-out spouse, "I don't remember Pat Boone saying that's what rock 'n roll was all about." Unfortunately, she cannot read lips and my protest was completely lost in the ongoing cacophony.

At length, Skid Row's barrage of trashy talk and death-defying decibels abated, and we were treated to the obligatory 45-minute wait while the stage was reset for the featured attraction. I can never understand why so much time and attention is given to this intermezzo in that all that is required in the way of instrumentation are extension cords and wall sockets.

During the interval the Bon Jovi roadies did what is benignly called "sound check" with recorded music. As best I can tell, this consists of nothing more than turning up the volume on the tractor-trailer size speakers to insure that the street lights dim as far as Marietta and that everyone in the first 20 rows of the Omni is bleeding steadily from the nose and ears.

Amid fireworks and blinding light, Bon Jovi suddenly materialized on stage. Except for their keyboard pummeler, who looked like the illicit love child of Phyllis Diller and the Phantom of the Opera, they were a far better looking bunch than Skid Row. Curiously, all of their t-shirts, posters and record albums featured the words "New Jersey" in letters of equal size and promience following "Bon Jovi." I have known many people from New Jersey but none who would admit it so readily. It is a well-documented fact that when the Playboy Clubs opened in New Jersey, the bunnies dressed in rat suits.

Though I had not heard any of their selections previously, I must confess that on balance their concert was a very entertaining and lively display. And, at times, their back beat got so basic that my toe began to tap involuntarily, causing the children in my vicinity to roll their eyes at me and gape as though Dame Margaret Rutherford had suddenly broken into a buck and wing.

As my grizzled spouse and I pulled the cotton from our ears and joined the sated crowd lowing toward the exits, it occurred to me that I still didn't know if Bon Jovi was the name of the lead singer or the name of the group. When I ventured to ask, my wife, who is so old that when she went to college foreign language was still a required course, she said tersely, "Bon Jovi is French for 'good Jovi.'" That was when I put the cotton back in my ears.

Robert L. Steed

February 17, 1989

To Mike Steed from Portugal: (5-20-71)

This is the greatest place
imaginable—the scenery is a
bit overwhelming and the
solitude unbelievable.
Everything reminds us of
Mexico. Lu blends in well—
wherever we go tourists
come up and ask her for
directions. People mostly
laugh and point at me.
Perhaps this is the first
double-knit lamé number
they have seen in the Old
World.

Bob

July 26, 1990

Kermit Birchfield, Esq.
Annisquam
Gloucester, Massachusetts

Dear K.B.:

I received a glowing account from Ned Hawie of their visit to Annisquam (Indian for "I gotta go").

Lu and I just got back from a Good Will Tour of France, Spain and Morocco and are now hunkered down awaiting the tidal wave of AMEX charges which are soon going to be crashing onto our fiscal shores. Lu almost cornered the market in Moroccan rugs but, just when they were getting really worried, a consortium of Arab sheiks and AmWay dealers broke her grip before they could get trapped in a short position. We don't have any floor space left and Lu is now cutting them up to use as antimacassars.

I'm enclosing for your refrigerator door a Frozen Moment in Time on the beach at Agadir. Shortly after the photo was made, a lifeguard told me to get a top for my bathing suit or get off the beach.

Until we see you again, I remain

Cute as a button,

Robert L. Steed

July 9, 1990

Mr. John J. McAtee, Jr.
Vice Chairman
Smith Barney Harris Upham
New York, New York

Dear Jack:

I read with interest in the *Wall Street Journal* of your new change of course and congratulate you and Smith Barney Harris Upham & Company on what I know will be a new career filled with challenge and success.

I'm still toiling in the municipal bond vineyards and, at 53 years old and having practiced since 1962, I relate in the strongest way to your refreshing career change. However, my goal has always been to gain employment as a stunt man in stag movies and I'm afraid I've let the moment pass. The competition is, as they say, getting too stiff.

Good luck in your new career.

With warmest regards, I am

Fading fast,

Robert L. Steed

July 12, 1990

Colonel Tony Privett
Business Maggot
Grizzard Enterprises, Inc.
Atlanta, Georgia

Dear Colonel:

Enclosed is my marker for $250 U.S. for the August 20 Scottish Rite Tournament.

If I find that you are getting a "taste" of this from Scottish Rite, it will severely shake my faith in you and crippled children everywhere. The thing that makes me a little suspicious is that this year, according to the entry form, the benefit is for the Scottish Rite Children's Hospital and "Georgia Handicapped Sportsman." The fact that "sportsman" is singular makes me think you may be representing a particular "Handicapped Sportsman" who will benefit from this enterprise. My guess is that you have set up a funny foundation for Lewis (Handicap: Body Rash of Unknown Origin) Grizzard or David (Handicap: Life-threatening Shanks) Boyd without their knowledge and are planning to do some serious skimming.

I am quick to admit that I don't have any hard evidence of any of this and it is based entirely on our past dealings. However, I did want to issue this warning that you and the entire enterprise are under scrutiny. (Scrutiny, a dancer at The Gold Club, could not be reached for comment.)

Until then, I am

Looking askance,

Robert L. Steed

July 9, 1990

Mr. James R. Newman
Assistant Vice President
Southern Bell
Atlanta, Georgia

Dear Jim:

You are a kind soul to send us the Vidalia onions. We had some of them fried up last night and they were even better than the Varsity's.

I've probably passed along Johnny B. Lastinger's story to you but if I haven't, it's worth repeating. Johnny B. told me that when his son John was quarterbacking Georgia in the Sugar Bowl, he and his wife, Lamb, went into Antoine's Restaurant for lunch and were confronted in the foyer by a typical Georgia Bulldog fan. He described the woman as being silver-haired, about 65 years old, smoking a cigarette and wearing every kind of Georgia Bulldog paraphernalia she could load onto herself, including a pair of silver lamé britches. He said that she had been drinking so much she looked like she was walking on a trampoline. She gave them an eye and asked, "Are y'all Bulldogs?" Johnny B. said that notwithstanding Lamb's nudge that he not get involved, he confessed they were. This caused the woman to ask him where in Georgia they were from and, when he said Valdosta, she shrieked, "*Valdosta!* Hot damn, I love them onions!"

We're just like she was; we love them onions!
With renewed thanks and warmest regards, I am

Plucky as ever,

Robert L. Steed

May 2, 1990

Ms. Barbara Forwald
Bianchi Travel Agency
Phoenix, Arizona

Re: *We're Off on the Road to Morocco*

Dear Barbara:

If Allison is to be believed (and the general feeling
is that he isn't), I am in your debt to the extent of
$5,618 (American). Allison is a master of short divi-
sion. Every time he divides, I wind up short. My
marker in that amount is enclosed.

Richard also passed along your speculation that
we might be able to get a goat for Lu in Morocco if we
could find a White Slaver with an anorexia fetish. I
won't rule it out until I see the goat. It reminds me of
the old story about the young man who came to an
older man and said, "I'd like to have your daughter for
my wife." The old man thought about it and replied,
"Well, bring your wife around and we'll talk about it."

This promises to be a very lively trip.

With warmest regards, I am

At the ready,

Robert L. Steed

June 13, 1990

Dr. Ferrol Sams
Sams Clinic
Fayetteville, Georgia

Dear Sambo:

You were a prince (though that does sound something like a German shepherd) to attend to me this morning on short notice, and I give you my warmest thanks for being so nice. I would have given you some American money as well but the cashier said the visit was on the house. This is genuinely appreciated but it does cut into some of my speech material (i.e., "I know a doctor who defines 'unnecessary surgery' as 'performing an operation when you don't even need the money'").

The Root Doctor, Mahaley [Lu Steed], was happy with and relieved by your diagnosis. I think she had dark and unhappy visions of my indisposition cutting into her freestyle shopping during the trip.

Thanks again and we'll see you when we get back. Until then, I am

Wheezing along,

Robert L. Steed

To Mike Steed from Morocco: (6-30-90)

Michael—

I've learned to speak a little Arabic. "Omar Shariff" means (1) "Clean up that camel and bring her to my tent," or (2) "I bid two clubs." If someone displeases you, say "Kiss my Aswan."

— Sheik Steed

July 6, 1990

Squire Barry Newman
Unlicensed Whittler
Buchanan, Georgia

Dear Barry:

Your last communique reached my office while I was with that 101 pounds of grit, gristle and ingratitude often identified as my wife on a Good Will Tour of France, Spain and Morocco.

Now I am wading through back mail, solicitations for political contributions and suggestions that I may have won various sweepstakes and waiting for a towering tidal wave of AMEX charges to sweep us off our fiscal feet.

Thanks for your letter to the editor. I agree with its premise that we Southerners run the risk of losing our heritage by mixing and intermarrying with what Lewis Grizzard calls "New Jersey Americans." In that connection, I just learned that the State of New Jersey has a new motto on its 1990 license plates. It asks simply, "What died?" I don't know if all of New Jersey is as bad as that string of cities on the Hudson, but I do remember that they made the waitresses in the Bayonne Playboy Club wear rat costumes.

With warmest regards, I am

Jet-lagged and tapped out,

Robert L. Steed

April 22, 1986

Ms. Carolyn Layfield
Columbus, Georgia

Dear Carolyn:

Your thoughtful husband has informed me that
you and he have been married for one-quarter of a
century, and he said that he wanted to commemorate
the event by presenting you with a book of letters from
friends and admirers. I am not surprised; he would go
to any length to come up with a cheap anniversary
present.

I can certainly understand why he asked me to
join in this enterprise. First, of course, he knows that
I love you dearly but, more to the point still, he knows
that I have, like you, been a victim of a long and
unhappy marriage myself. I can relate in the strongest
way to the living hell that is involved in spending 25
years with someone who looks like a poster child for
anorexia while everything on your body gets bigger
and closer to the ground. (Well, almost everything.)

I can remember the days at Mercer when your love
(and Christian sympathy) for Marty was so strong
that you endured the scorn and derision of your
sorority sisters who said that he looked like a remnant
of the Bataan Death March and that his ears caused
him to resemble a taxicab with both doors open.

I can remember too how proud you were of him
when we Phi Delta Thetas wrapped those ears in tin-

foil and used him as an antenna for our television set. We could pick up stations as far away as Quebec.

I admired your courage as you helped him avoid military service by hiding him under the porch of your family's home and later, when he claimed to be pregnant, doing the right thing and marrying him.

I can remember how wonderfully supportive you were during his career as a young lawyer in Atlanta where he quickly established a reputation in the area of witnessing wills and notarizing deeds. You were always so supportive and had an ever kind and encouraging word for him. I have often quoted you when discussing him with other people. You always said, "Marty's a helluva lot smarter than he looks." This was at a time when the rest of us thought that the only thing that would ever be distinguished about him was his Adam's apple.

You have been patient and long-suffering while he jacked around with merging Columbus and Moscogee County, messed around in Younger Lawyers Section and ABA politics, foisted Bobby Hydrick off on an unsuspecting public, backed Brother Bush, and took on any other form of human endeavor that would permit him to avoid spending an honest day's work at his practice.

You have borne him four marvelous children who, because of his contribution to the gene pool, were all able to get in Auburn and, I am sure, will be able to get into college after they graduate.

After a quarter of a century of sacrifice and unhappiness, you find yourself in the same unhappy dilemma that I am in—your mate has progressed from a bundle of gristle, mean spirits and ingratitude to the point of being just plain pitiful and you feel that all of your friends would blame you for leaving. I urge you to be philosophic about your situation and keep alert to the possibilities for some good "side action." (I'll have to be frank and tell you that I haven't had much success in this regard. A friend recently asked me if I "was getting any on the side" and I had to confess that I didn't even know they had moved it.)

Keep sweet and pretty and know that you are loved and admired by —

Yours truly,

Robert L. Steed

December 26, 1990

Mr. Michael D. Easterly
Managing Director
Morgan Keegan & Company, Inc.
Atlanta, Georgia

Dear Mike:

Many thanks for the Confederate corn bread fixings. Lu Steed has a black belt in corn bread and will have this in a skillet before the week is out.

The Confederate edition reminds me of the old joke about the Confederate veteran who, long after the Great War, was reminded by one of his former Union Army adversaries of the general pre-war boast by the Confederate that, "We can whip the Yankees with corn stalks." When the Union veteran reminded him of the ultimate result, the old Confederate soldier replied, "And we could have, by dammit. You Yankees just wouldn't fight with corn stalks."

In any case, I'm glad to have this Yuletide token, corny or not.

With warmest regards, I am

The short, wide, white-haired one,

Robert L. Steed

December 13, 1990

Executive Committee
Atlanta Lawyers Club, Inc.
Atlanta, Georgia

Laurie and Gentlemen:

That quivering mass of nerve endings which passes for a trial lawyer, Paul M. (for "Manic") Hawkins, has proposed for membership in our exalted precincts his young associate, Thomas F. Wamsley, Jr., Esq. (I can picture the scene now as Hawkins summons young Wamsley to his chambers and, looking over both shoulders, says conspiratorially, "Wamsley, I'm putting you up for the Lawyers Club in lieu of a raise and bonus, of course. Keep this business under your hat as I wouldn't want to upset the other associates.")

The purpose of this letter is to enthusiastically endorse the proposal on behalf of young Wamsley. I know him well and commend him to you as a fine young lawyer, a golfer of considerable skill and a congenial prospect who will add a measure of youth and vitality to our ranks. He is a law graduate of the University of South Carolina and a Vanderbilt undergraduate, attending college with and serving as a responsible role model for my son, Joshua Steed, who, as best we can tell, was setting intercollegiate records for parking tickets and bank overdrafts.

Tom has a wife, Jenny, and a child, Tee, which would, in my judgment, serve as a hedge against the possibility that he might leave town abruptly with an outstanding balance for dues or drink tabs.

I commend him to you with much enthusiasm and hope you will be able to give him prompt and positive consideration.

With warmest regards, I am

Reasonably alert,

Robert L. Steed

November 21, 1990

Thomas S. Currier, Esq.
New York, New York

Dear Tom:

I'm sorry that I won't be able to make your mustering out party on December 7 but think the date shows a keen sense of timing. There was, of course, the unpleasantness with the Japanese on that date, the legendary Winecoff Hotel fire in Atlanta, and now a significant loss to the active Bar.

When I recall your auspicious start which, if memory serves, involved reading Cliff Notes on Fundamentals of Municipal Bond Law Preparatory to Becoming an Instant Bond Daddy, I am tempted to paraphrase Sir Winston:

"Never in the history of tax-free endeavor have so few said so much knowing so little."

But, as one who is himself approaching the twilight of a mediocre career, I can also paraphrase the Great Emancipator with equal enthusiasm:

"You can fool some of the people all of the time and all of the people some of the time and, when you think about it, them ain't bad odds."

I hope your retirement is filled with happy days, sexual abandon and interesting enterprise.

With all good wishes, I am

Increasingly sedentary,

Robert L. Steed

January 10, 1991

Mrs. Nimrod Frazer
Montgomery, Alabama

Dear Sweet Thing,

You must have learned that during my last physical exam I was told that my cholesterol level was getting dangerously low. A "better than sex chocolate cake" is just what the doctor ordered. My doctor ordered sex too (with a medical technician) and his wife ordered him out of the house. He fell back in love in her lawyer's office when he heard how much it was going to cost him to trade her in on the technician.

Lu and I got on the outside of some of the cake last night and it made my face break out before I went to bed. I'm laying in a supply of Clearasil as I don't plan to give up on the cake.

Lu says you'll give us the recipe and she certainly wants it. I suggested she mix equal amounts of creamery butter, sugar and chocolate together and thought she would come pretty close.

With hugs and kisses, I remain

Cute as a button,

Robert L. Steed

January 24, 1991

Mr. Robert W. Dhue
President
Atlanta Coliseum, Inc.
The Omni
Atlanta, Georgia

Dear Bob:

Enclosed is my marker (if it doesn't go through the first time, just keep trying to cash it) for $157.50 covering seven tickets to the Randy Travis show. If you will have Kathy call my secretary, Yvonne "I Didn't Go To Marsh Business College For Six Months To Learn How To Bring You Coffee" McMillian, she will send one of our winged messengers to bring them back, thus avoiding the risk that the U.S. Postal Service might not deliver them in the current fiscal year.

I hope that Randy is at the top of his game, but we'll have lots of fun in any event.

With warmest regards, I am

Just an old song nobody sings anymore,

Robert L. Steed

November 27, 1990

Dear Fellow Members of the
Walter F. George School of Law
Class of 1961

The folks at our *alma mater* have contacted me
pointing out that 1991 marks the 30th anniversary of
our graduation. They suggest that we might want to
celebrate this occasion with a social function in connection with Law Day, which is scheduled for Friday,
April 12.

I expressed some doubts, pointing out that most of
our class were scattered in detoxification centers and
nursing homes throughout South Georgia and North
Florida or were practicing under assumed names.

They persisted, pointing out that the Law Day
speaker for '91 will be William Webster, the Director of
the CIA. The schedule also includes a morning alumni
meeting, the luncheon at which Judge Webster will
speak, an afternoon CLE program, and an early evening cocktail party. With all of these blandishments
and an increasing awareness that many in our class
will not be mobile for much longer, I was persuaded to
send you this inquiry to delve into your interest at the
prospect of a reunion. Please fill it in and return it in
the envelope provided.

With warmest regards, I am

Increasingly jowly,

Robert L. Steed

January 31, 1991

Ms. Patricia W. Bass
Assistant Dean
Walter F. George School of Law
Mercer University
Macon, Georgia

Dear Tricia:

Enclosed is a letter for distribution to the Class of 1961.

The collective response of our class reminds me of the old story about the pollster who called someone and asked, "What is your reaction to the charge that our country is in the grip of ignorance and apathy?" The respondent replied, "I don't know and I don't give a damn."

Yours sincerely,

Robert L. Steed

February 5, 1991

Dear Fellow Class Members of 1961:

Based on the collective response to my recent inquiry as to whether members of the class would like to hold a 30th reunion in connection with this year's Law Day, I would have to say that you were absolutely underwhelmed at the prospect. We had nine affirmatives and two negatives. Of the affirmatives, four were anonymous (forestalling any criticism that might be incurred by someone who said the reunion was a good idea but later failed to show up).

Accordingly, I have cancelled the private dining room at the Nu-Way (they were crestfallen as they had planned a special entree just for our reunion — "Wieners Wellington"), and told the exotic dancer I had engaged that she would not have to ask the Waffle House to let her off that evening. She and I will work out the matter of the deposit I advanced.

With warmest regards, I am

Mildly disappointed,

Robert L. Steed

March 1, 1991

Mr. Duncan Dew (formerly
  Lead Singer of Duncan Dew
  and the Dropouts)
Florence, South Carolina 29505

Dear Squire Dew:

Many thanks for your recent note dealing with Law Day, your flying lessons and sexual opportunities at the Waffle House.

I neglected to mention in my letter to the Class of 1961 that the most important reason for coming to this year's Law Day is to see my portrait which was installed outside the Moot Courtroom upon my having retired after five years as Chairman of Tatnall Tech. I can only imagine what it would mean to someone like you to appear in a photograph with me flanking my portrait and, for a specified substantial donation to the Law School, that option will be available to those who come to Law Day 1991.

As for your flying lessons, I am not impressed. They taught the kamikaze to fly too . . . they just didn't teach them to land.

As to your alleged eagerness for slap and tickle opportunities at the Waffle House, I have learned from frequent phone calls from Elaine (and the poor dear is on the phone to me all the time), that the waffles at your house never get quite done. She said frankly that your sexual encounters were getting so increasingly infrequent that you sometimes forgot who was sup-

posed to tie the other one up. She lamented that your
FBI-agent handcuffs so frequently used in the early
days of the marriage were now rusting on a peg in the
garage. She also suspects you've been "dressing up"
in her clothes when she goes to the mall so watch
youself.

On a completely different subject, I was startled
last evening in my office to get a phone call from the
ever-morose J. Milton Harrison (former winner of the
Milton Clark Barwick Practice and Pleading Award),
who informed me that he was in town to interview
with a Republican Judicial Screening Committee.
Apparently he is interested in becoming a U.S. Judge. I
must admit that this is a prospect so terrifying that I
can barely consider it without recoiling or bursting
into laughter. It is quite something to have someone
you have known for a long time call and, out of the
blue, confess that they have always been a Republican.
He certainly didn't exhibit any of those tendencies in
Law School but then you can never tell. Many Republi-
cans actually marry and have children.

With warmest good wishes to your Sweet Spouse, I
am

Very important,

Robert L. Steed

February 13, 1991

Executive Committee
Lawyers Club of Atlanta, Inc.
Atlanta, Georgia

Dear Colleagues:

My friend (well, actually, he's just an acquaintance), Gary M. Sams, has recommended Norma W. Bergman for resident membership in our esteemed and elite circle, and the purpose of this note is to warmly endorse that proposition.

In my judgment, Norma would add considerable luster to our roster. She is Corporate Counsel to Academy Insurance Group, Inc., and is an Emory law graduate. Her undergraduate degree is from the University of Rochester (so named because of a handsome endowment left to the school by Jack Benny's longtime chauffeur).

What some of you may not know is that Norma's father-in-law, Frank Jenkins, joined my wife and me in a tasteful double-ring ceremony in the Bowdon Methodist Church over 32 years ago. The fact that I am able to mention this so calmly offers ringing proof, if proof is wanted, of the fact that I am not one to hold a grudge.

If any doubt Norma's ability to survive the chaos, loud talk and confusion which characterize our monthly meetings, I would only point out that for eight years, she was a member of the DeKalb County Board of Education, serving as Chairman for two of those

years. She performed wonderfully under those circumstances, and I think she will do even better at our
gatherings as drinking is not only permitted, it is
actively encouraged.

With warmest regards, I am

Subject to wild mood swings,

Robert L. Steed

May 1, 1986

Mr. C. David Butler
Alston & Bird
Atlanta, Georgia

Dear David (and Susie):

You two have really rung Lu's "gustatory" bell
with the *White Trash Cookbook*.

If Bowdon, Georgia, had tracks, Lu's family would
be on the wrong side of them. They are as country as
cornbread and as sorry as gully dirt. If not for me, Lu
would still be selling scuppernongs off the back of a
pickup truck or reading palms in a dingy house trailer
on the Bankhead Highway. ("Madam Lu — calls your
friends and enemies by name.")

I have personally seen her crumble up cornbread
in a tall glass, fill it with buttermilk and eat it with an
iced tea spoon. I tell you, it's not a pretty sight.

Just the other night she was complaining because
Kroger didn't carry her favorite brand of salmon —
Double "Q." She is truly the Julia Child of country
cuisine.

The only down side of your thoughtfulness is that
the pictures make her homesick for her peckerwood
relatives and, as they don't have a telephone, we'll
probably have to go home and see them. I always dread
this as they are forever hitting on me for money and
think that my blue dress shirts with the white collars
are "factory seconds."

You two are as sweet as you are fecund and we both love being thought of even if the stimulus was "White Trash."

With warmest regards, I am

Easily aroused,

Robert L. Steed

*While Atlanta was rallying support in its bid to host the 1996
Summer Olympics, the City of San Francisco was involved in a
political squabble which resulted in the San Francisco Board of
Supervisors approving their Organizing Committee's bid for the
1996 Summer Games only if the Organizing Committee agreed to
certain stipulations aimed at appeasing the city's homosexual
community. Steed, having been the victim of hostile letters to the
editor after commenting on a San Francisco Gay Rights Parade
he observed during the 1984 Democractic Convention, obviously
decided that cowardice was the better part of valor and offered
some column ideas on the San Francisco matter to columnist
Lewis Grizzard through his manager, Tony Privett.*

March 10, 1988

Mr. Tony Privett
Grizzard Enterprises, Inc.
Atlanta, Georgia

Dear Colonel Parker:

Enclosed is a cutting (I've been to England a time
or two) from yesterday's *Constitution* indicating that
in connection with the site of the upcoming Olympics
there are "Gay demands attached to Bay Area bid." I
suspect that's not the only thing they're attached to
but, putting that aside, it occurred to me that, lacking
the courage myself to do battle with the Pink Panthers,

this dispatch might be grist for Uncle Lewis' comedy mill.

One of the conditions was that the U. S. Olympic Committee allows organizers of the "Gay Games" to use the word "Olympics" and, of course there are more.

The possibilities seem rampant here:

(1) Grizzard could speculate about new games to be added as a result of the demands, i.e., the "hop, skip and jump" competition could be changed to the "mince, skip and swish" competition or a "skip, goose and leap-frog" event.

(2) They could add a make-up competition.

(3) They could give a "Miss Congeniality" award.

(4) At least one of the relay teams could be required to use electric vibrators instead of batons.

(5) The existing penalty in relays and other races for following too close could be abolished.

(6) A grape or Kleenex-squashing competition could be added to the games. There could be posters featuring a precious-looking athlete saying "Hi, I'm Bruce, and I'll be your shot-putter today."

(7) They could have a smurf shot put competition.

Also worthy of comment is the fact that the San Francisco resolution asked the USOC to support reformation of U. S. immigration laws that permit denial of entry to alien homosexuals. I know E.T. walked funny, but I didn't know he was light in his loafers (or should we say "light in his Reeboks").

The mind boggles at all this, but then my mind boggles so easily.

With warmest regards to you, Uncle Lewis and all under your protection, I remain

Above the fruited plain,

Robert L. Steed

October 8, 1987

Hon. Mel Hawkins
Dahlonega, Georgia

Dear Mel:

Those ever alert folks at the *Atlanta Constitution* just forwarded me two letters you had sent to me in care of them—one in March of 1987 and the other in September of 1987. I can only assume that because of the expense of forwarding the things, they like to wait until they have a batch.

I like the idea of mixed doubles on Live Atlanta Wrestling. We might even talk the Playboy Channel into featuring them in the buff or, as Lewis Grizzard says, "nekkid."

I very much appreciated the photo from the *Market Bulletin* showing Mrs. Marva Jones and her stupendous squash. It reminded me of a time when I was back in high school and a stripper had been signed for the Burger Inn in Tallapoosa. She was similarly endowed and the owner of the night spot asked her manager what kind of dance she did. The manager said, "Dance? She don't *dance*. She just crawls out on the stage and tries to stand up."

So that you will remember what I am replying to, I am sending back your missives.

With warm regards, I remain

Easily addled,

Robert L. Steed

December 9, 1988

Mr. and Mrs. Hughes Spalding
Senior Citizens
Atlanta, Georgia

Dear Spaldings:

As we don't have any Junior Leaguers in the Bond
Department, it falls my lot to write the thank-you note
for your thoughtful Christmas washtub filled with
popcorn.

It is very timely. I had just lost a few pounds
because of the sustained romancing of my kidney
stone and this will certainly take care of that. . . .

With renewed thanks and warmest regards, I am

Munching away,

Robert L. Steed

September 9, 1988

Mr. Ben Hudson
Hudson & Marshall
Macon, Georgia

Dear Ben:

This is to confirm that we are on for lunch and golf at the Capital City Club on Tuesday, November 22.

[Lewis] Grizzard is a mercurial and undependable character given to wild mood swings. Because of this, we will likely reschedule this event four or five times before we finally nail it down, but for purposes of present planning, November 22 seems to hit everybody's spot.

You will be able to recognize me easily as I will be dressed as a Shriner after having just delivered a speech the night before to the National Convention of the Order of the Eastern Star.

Oh, another thing about Grizzard, he, like the Prince of Wales, likes to make big bets but never pays off when he loses. He also moves the ball in the rough, talks during his own backswing and at the first sign of lightning leaves the golf course much in the manner of a mailbag leaving a rail siding. Other than that, he is a blooming delight.

Looking forward to seeing you on the 22nd, if that date holds, I am

Quick on the backswing,

Robert L. Steed

The following is a response by Steed to a letter from his perpetual pen pal, Barry Newman, which enclosed a photograph of Newman.

July 7, 1988

Mr. Barry Newman
Buchanan, Georgia

Dear Barry:

Thanks so much for the picture. It explains everything. Immediately after I received it I contacted Ferrante and Teicher and they verified that one of them was your father. However, they wouldn't be more specific than that. Based on the facial hair and outfit, I'm thinking Teicher.

Watch out for low-flying Democrats.

With best regards, I remain

Constantly befuddled,

Robert L. Steed

June 28, 1988

Mr. Jack N. Sibley
Freeman & Hawkins
Atlanta, Georgia

Dear Jack:

Thanks for your note saying that you are now with Freeman & Hawkins. You have thrown in with a mighty good bunch of folks and I know it will be a pleasant and prosperous professional alliance.

Of course, I know the venerable and eponymous founders of the firm but generally discount them as so little blood is getting to their brains these days that I'm sure euthanasia is the first alternative contemplated by your firm's compensation committee when dealing with either of them.

Hoping this finds you well and happy with plenty of spring in your step, I am

Yours sincerely,

Robert L. Steed

February 9, 1990

Mr. James L. Johnson
Pandick Atlanta
Atlanta, Georgia

Dear J. J.:

Lu Steed sends you with her compliments a copy of "Lonesome Dove." Actually, I was the one who sat through three nights of televiewing editing out the commercials, but she likes to take credit for sending it to you, so there you are.

If you come up with any extra Masters tickets, let me know. However, don't go to any trouble because Lu and I are covered for one day, but my request is for all of my grown children who are always scratching for tickets. They can go on short notice but don't neglect anybody important in their behalf. I just told them I would put some lines in the water. I feel like Big Bird. Every time I fly back to our nest, there they all are with their mouths open hungry for hard-to-get tickets.

With best regards, I am

Always looking for an angle,

Robert L. Steed

February 5, 1990

Mr. and Mrs. Howard Smith
Malibu, California

Dear Howard and Jane:

Lu and I enjoyed being with you folks Friday evening and hope we will have other opportunities to get
together soon.

As promised (or was it "threatened"), I am sending you a copy of that brightly blazing star in the
American literary firmament, *The Sass Menagerie*. So
Lu won't feel completely left out, I am sending along a
couple of copies of her catalogs in the hope that you
can find her some famous movie star who wants to be
painted with her/his automobile. Given the predisposi-
tion of Californians to move about on wheels, I think
this is not an altogether unlikely prospect. I still
remember a cover I saw years ago on *New West* which
featured a rich-looking mother standing beside her
teenage son who was in a wheel chair. The caption
read, "Of course he can walk. Thank goodness, he
doesn't *have* to."

With best regards to you both, I am

Subject to wild mood swings,

Robert L. Steed

September 14, 1987

Lou Green, Esq.
Editor
Younger Lawyers Section Newsletter

Dear Lou,

You have asked me to write a few words on the history of the Younger Lawyers Section Newsletter and I am happy to oblige. However, as so little blood is reaching my brain these days, I must say in advance that anything I offer is sure to be a bit spotty.

In 1961, upon graduating from Walter F. George School of Law at Mercer University, I was given a job as Clerk on the Supreme Court of Georgia (I subsequently quit in a fit of pique when I learned the other Clerks were being paid). Despite that high station, I quickly fell in with low company, specifically, Charles M. Driebe, who was then performing similar clerking duties on the Georgia Court of Appeals. Driebe, known at the time by his small but dedicated group of followers as "Captain Swarthy," was, by his own admission, a high-ranking official of the world powerful Younger Lawyers Section which had been founded in 1947 in order to give younger lawyers something to do with their hands.

Through large measures of guile and cunning, Driebe had managed to insinuate himself as Secretary of the Section and, in an egregious effort at self-aggrandizement, had created the Younger Lawyers Section Newsletter as a vehicle to bleat his own meager accomplishments (giving plaques to all other young lawyers who might help him gain his political goals and attending any bar meeting from Rabun Gap to Tybee Light which offered free cocktails).

Driebe edited the Newsletter himself from late 1961 through May of 1962 when he became aware of the fact that his relentless self-laudatory prose was testing the collective gag reflex of the Bar Association in general. Sensing in me a naive soul who would not think to question his motives, he made me a Faustian proposal which involved making me his successor as Editor of the Newsletter on the condition that each subsequent edition feature a photograph of him on every other page. True to my word, I brought out the August 1963 Newsletter (Volume 3, No. 1) with a photo of Driebe on the cover and inaugurated the first in a series of biographical sketches aimed at acquainting members of the Younger Lawyers Section with their new officers. An excerpt from Driebe's sketch will serve to illustrate the tone of his bio and those that followed:

"Driebe's family background is steeped in legal tradition. Two of his cousins can boast of never having missed a Perry Mason Show; an older brother was introduced into evidence by the defense in the Scopes Monkey Trail; a distant relation, Justice Hugo Driebe of the U. S. Supreme Court, made legal history by declaring World War II unconstitutional; a maiden aunt, Brunhilde Driebe, works quietly in Catoosa County circulating a petition to free Sacco and Vanzetti (when questioned about her crusade, Miss Driebe said simply, "They never done it."); and a step-brother who has dedicated his life to finding Judge Crater."

Lamentably, the Pulitzer Committee chose not to expand its annual awards to include a newsletter category, and thus our publication never really received the acclaim it richly deserved. However, like a raging virus, it caught on and has continued to this day faithfully reporting the comings and goings of plaque presenters throughout the State of Georgia, spouting nonsense and aberrant attempts at humor and, on rare occasions, printing some news of real interest and relevance to Georgia lawyers. By way of example (and there are precious few) the enclosed photo from the lead article of the April, 1963, Newsletter represents a particularly historic frozen moment in time when, on March 11, 1963, the bill to incorporate the Georgia Bar Associaton as a unified State Bar of Georgia was signed into law by then Governor Carl E. Sanders.

Throughout the twenty-six year history of the YLS Newsletter, which has been filled with highs and lows (the term of William D. Barwick as Editor is generally conceded to be the nadir of its existence), its tone and tenor has consistently reflected the continuing commitment of Georgia younger lawyers to Bar activities. That commitment was probably best expressed by the immortal bard of the Pelham Bar, the Honorable Fred B. Hand, Jr., who, from a recumbent position on the back seat floor of a Yellow Cab in front of the old DeSoto Hilton Hotel in Savannah, was heard to say:

"Bar meetings are not all fun
Take pictures, get awards and jaw.
But for all the hard drinking,
They beat hell out of thinking,
Real work or practicing law."

There was some other stuff, but I've forgotten that. With best regards, I remain

Soft and cuddly,

Robert L. Steed.

P.S. Charles Driebe was thought by many of us to be destined for further greatness, but stronger anti-Arab feeling during the oil crisis and the fact that he moved to Jonesboro, Georgia, caused him to fade into obscurity. He is now head of the Clayton County PLO and ekes out a living as a part-time lookout for a massage parlor on Highway 41 South.

December 18, 1989

Mr. Jim Cowart
Dunwoody, Georgia

Dear Jim:

One of our mail room folks came into my office with a big package which bore this legend— "JOLLY NUT." I couldn't figure out at first whether that was how they addressed it and it automatically came to me or if somebody was violating my trademark.

A closer look revealed a very fine gift of pecans from you and they are received with warm thanks.

Lu's thanks will be even warmer as she is the "pecan queen." She loves to eat them and loves to cook with them, and I send her warm thanks as well.

Yours sincerely,

Robert L. Steed

December 20, 1989

Mr. Francis E. King
Merrill Lynch Capital Markets
New York, New York

Dear Frank:

I am sending this to you to thank Merrill Lynch
Capital Markets for the marvelous pocket calendar
which I received this morning. It was accompanied by
a card but the signature appears to be in a foreign (or
perhaps extraterrestrial) script.

The best our cryptograph unit could come up with
was (1) "J. T. Dumbee, Jr."; (2) "T. L. Toumbe, Jr.";
or (3) "JOHO Umbe, Jr." I enclose a photocopy of the
card so you can have a chance at cracking the code.

In any event, I sincerely appreciate being on the
list and thank you for any part you might have had in
getting me there.

With warmest good wishes, I am

Still puzzled,

Robert L. Steed

The following is a reply by Steed to a lawyer friend in Raleigh, North Carolina, who invited Steed to be his houseguest when speaking to the North Carolina Bar Association.

September 9, 1988

V. Lane Wharton, Jr., Esq.
Hunter & Wharton
Raleigh, North Carolina

Dear Lane:

What a treat to hear from you. I have checked and our schedule will permit Lu, the children, several small animals and me to have at least three meals, put up at your house and perhaps organize from you a small loan of some "walking around money."

Actually, we have to forego that happy prospect in that the State Bar has already reserved the Conjugal Visit Suite at the Motel 8 on the Zebulon by-pass for us. I would pass it up in favor of your kind invitation but Lu has never seen action on a waterbed and, as you can imagine, she's not getting any younger. You will be shocked when you see her in October, but I continue to take her with me on speaking engagements as she is still able to cut up my meat and count drinks for me during the cocktail hour. She really should be in a home, but I promised the children to keep her with us as long as we can.

Lu and I would like to organize a visit with you and Linda, but our visit is complicated by the fact

that—this may be more than you want to know—
Georgia Steed is marrying a young lawyer here in
Atlanta whose father is a Womble, Carlyle attorney,
Charles Vance. Mr. and Mrs. Vance are coming (with
gritted teeth, I rather imagine) to Raleigh to hear and
see me expose myself. Fortunately, the wedding will
have taken place some twelve days earlier, so the
damage I can inflict by reason of my speech on this
happy union is limited. In any case, we are obliged to
parlay with them before and after the event, but I hope
we can get together with you for at least a drink to
catch up on your domestic affairs. I'll give you a call
early during the week of October 27 when I have a
clearer picture of what is expected of us by our in-laws-
to-be.

With best regards, I remain

Subject to wild mood swings,

Robert L. Steed

June 7, 1989

Mr. Henry Yaris
Product Manager/Dewars
Dallas, Texas

Dear Mr. Yaris:

Mr. Howard Feldman was good enough to give me your name as the appropriate Dewars contact for the subject matter of this communication.

I am sure you have an advertising agency that, among other things, processes zany letters like this one. As I do not know who that might be, I am sending this blind nomination to your attention with the request that you forward it to the appropriate person for such consideration as it may merit.

I have long been interested in your Dewar's Profile advertising theme and wish to nominate for a profile my wizened wife, who is as unique in her way as your fine whiskey.

She is a serious painter with a most unusual selection of subjects. Although slight in stature (I have characterized her as "101 pounds of grit, gristle and ingratitude"), she paints very large canvasses featuring 18-wheelers, truck stops and those who frequent them. I am enclosing catalogs of two of her most recent shows which will give you some idea of the subjects of her large acrylic paintings. She is also an avid gardener, magazine reader and is to malapropisms what Michael Milken was to junk bonds. I am convinced they broke the mold before they made her.

Beyond all that, she is a dog-loyal imbiber of Dewar's White Label Scotch Whiskey and will frown and flare her nostrils menacingly should I make any attempt to palm less worthy brands off on her.

I nominate her for serious consideration for a Dewar's Profile and, to give you an added measure of insight into this unique personality I am proposing to flog the sale of your spirits, I enclose a collection of some of my scribblings, *Money, Power and Sex (A Self-Help Guide for All Ages)*, which features some added relevant revelations as to her quirky nature.

With husbandly chutzpah, I am

Yours sincerely,

Robert L. Steed

April 2, 1991

Personal

(SEXUALLY EXPLICIT MATERIAL ENCLOSED.
TO BE OPENED ONLY BY THE ADDRESSEE.)

Mr. Lewis Grizzard
Southern Literary Icon
Atlanta, Georgia

Dear Uncle Lewis:

Lu Steed was recently showing a young lady around our house and they came to the painting she did some years back of a black woman— "Big Helen." Lu recalled wistfully and in some detail just how Helen helped raise our three dependents and extolled her virtues to the heavens. The young lady, obviously moved, asked Lu if Helen was dead and Lu replied, "No, but she can't be reached by phone." She looked at Lu like a dog does when you say something strange to it, but by then Lu had moved serenely to the next painting.

After trying unsuccessfully for three days to reach you by phone at your Ansley Park Redoubt, I am convinced that you are a lot like Big Helen.

This is a multipurpose alert covering the following grounds:

(1) Our Alabama friend, Thomas Harris called me to say he understands you're bringing your Live Animal Act to Montgomery, Alabama, on Sunday, April 28,

and he wanted me to extend to you an invitation to play the Montgomery Country Club that afternoon if you cared to. As an option, he offered the lush fairways of Shoal (now pr. "Soul") Creek in nearby Birmingham. I told him I couldn't speak for you (and added helpfully that sometimes very late in the evening you have difficulty speaking for yourself) but promised to pass along the invitation.

(2) The redoubtable Sambo called to extend an invitation to play in a "Little School Golf Tournament" at Whitewater Creek on Monday, June 3. I told him I would go if you would go and volunteered to drive you there in my new Motor Coach. He says we will not have to pay as it is a celebrity golf tournament and we are celebrities. You may be a celebrity but Claude Perry recently invited me to come as a celebrity to a Heart Fund Dinner in Cartersville. I stood around all evening being widely unrecognized until finally a woman came up to Lu and me and said, "You're the lady that paints the trucks, aren't you?"

I know this long letter has been an ordeal for you and can only imagine how tired your lips must be at this point. However, I am looking north from our new offices in the 191 Tower and hoping to see some white plumes from your Prado chimney.

With warm good wishes, I am

Fairly tired myownself,

Robert L. Steed

Squire Barry Newman
Unlicensed Whittler and
  Back Stoop Philosopher
Buchanan, Georgia

Dear Squire Newman:

Thanks for your latest communique.

I have indeed heard that my ancestral home, Bowdon, Georgia, has a golf course. I think it is called the Bowdon National Golf Club, Bait Shop and Video Rental. They were going to call it "Bowdon *Country* Club" but thought that would be redundant.

It has been interesting to observe the ease with which Bowdon's residents have shifted from their traditional sporting pursuits — frog gigging, possum hunting and arm-wrasslin' — to the more sophisticated pursuit of golf. The pockets on those bib overalls are wonderful for balls, golf tees, etc. and when the pants legs are tucked into a pair of baseball socks, they really do look like plus-fours from a distance.

On another subject, you may be (check one: ___ amused, ___ appalled, ___ absolutely indifferent) to learn that my crafty publishers, Longstreet Press (wedding announcements, lost dog posters, sex manuals and works of the occult), have determined to inflict a collection of my letters on an unsuspecting public and that a number of those letters are replies to your notes over recent years.

My darkest fear is that this dubious effort will result in towering stacks of remaindered books in bookstores everywhere or, worse yet, in landfills everywhere. Notwithstanding my persistent expressions of apprehension to them, the publishers remain supremely confident that they can sell a creditable number of what I consider to be a black hole in the literary ozone. We'll see.

I'll try my best to get them to spring for a free promotional copy for you but although the top knocker of the outfit, Claude ("Just Call Me Chuck") Perry looks like a second-string Santa Claus that might be hired by a cheap department store, he is as tight-fisted as anyone I have ever known.

Just keep your eye out for your rural free delivery mail carrier and hope for the best.

With warm good wishes, I am

At the end of my literary rope,

Robert L. Steed